THE

DORSET YEAR BOOK FOR 2020

ONE HUNDRED AND ELEVENTH YEAR OF ISSUE

First published in Great Britain in 2019 by The Society of Dorset Men

A CIP catalogue record for this book is available from the British Library.

Paperback ISBN No.: 578-0-9926594-86

Price £8.00

Edited by Nicholas Wright

Printed and bound in Great Britain by
Print Team (Dorset) Limited
www.printteam.co.uk

Cover photo: "Reedy Ditch Waterfall at Portland Bill after heavy summer rain".
Photo by Edgar Moxom.

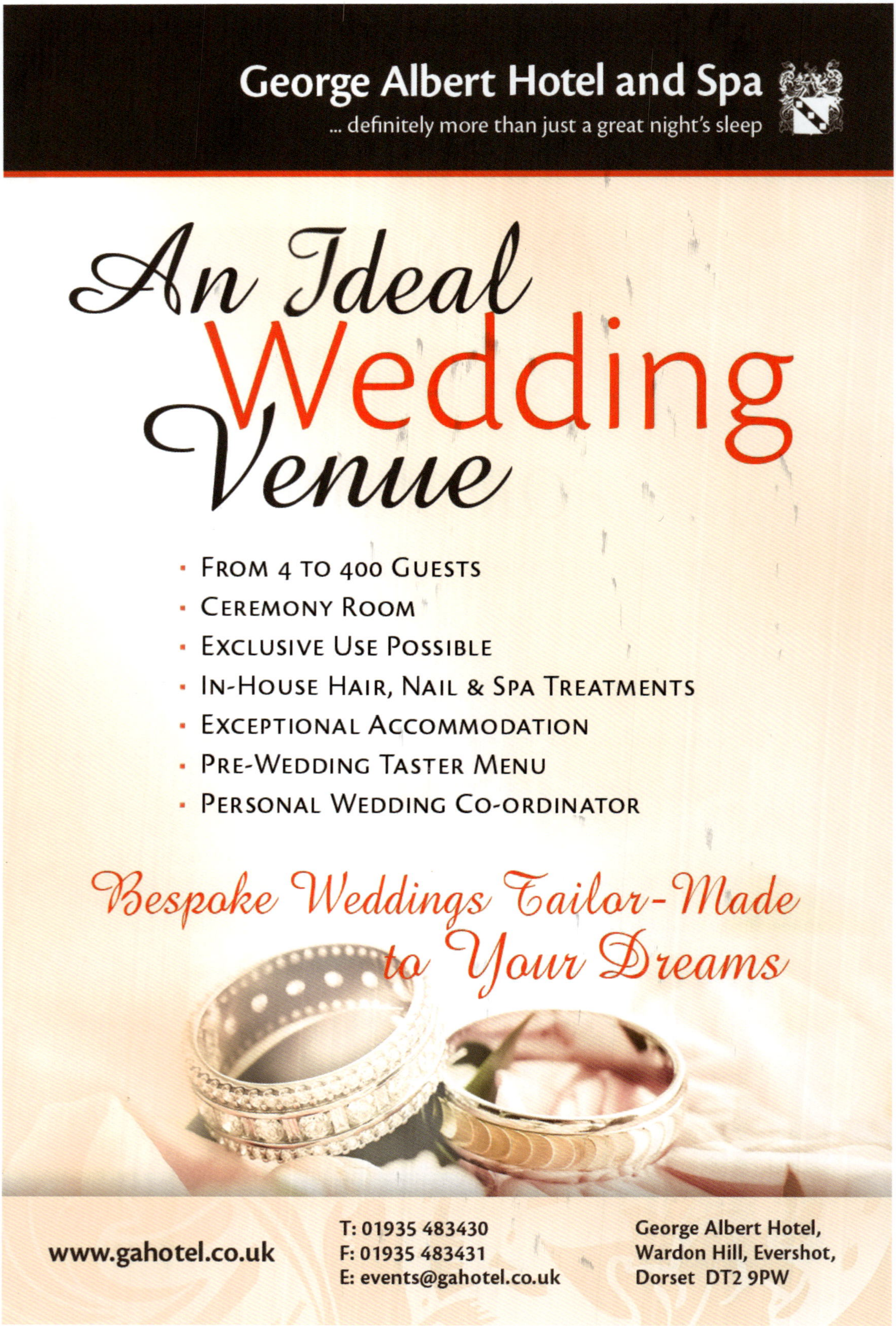
George Albert Hotel and Spa
... definitely more than just a great night's sleep
An Ideal Wedding Venue
· From 4 to 400 Guests
· Ceremony Room
· Exclusive Use Possible
· In-House Hair, Nail & Spa Treatments
· Exceptional Accommodation
· Pre-Wedding Taster Menu
· Personal Wedding Co-ordinator
Bespoke Weddings Tailor-Made to Your Dreams
www.gahotel.co.uk
T: 01935 483430
F: 01935 483431
E: events@gahotel.co.uk
George Albert Hotel,
Wardon Hill, Evershot,
Dorset DT2 9PW

THE SOCIETY OF DORSET MEN

FOUNDED JULY 7th, 1904

'A Silver Tower Dorset Red Banner Bears'

"WHO'S A-FEAR'D?"

President:
LORD FELLOWES OF WEST STAFFORD, DL

Deputy Presidents:
SIR ANTHONY JOLLIFFE, GBE, DL, D.Sc, D.Mus
DR. PAUL ATTERBURY, B.A. FRSA

Past Presidents:
SIR FREDERICK TREVES, BART, GCVO, CB, LLD, 1904 - 1907
THOMAS HARDY, OM, LITT.D, JP, 1907 - 1909
COLONEL JOHN MOUNT BATTEN, CB, 1909 - 1911
COLONEL SIR ROBERT WILLIAMS, BART, VD, 1911 - 1913
SIR STEPHEN COLLINS, JP, 1913 - 1915
JOHN CASTLEMAN SWINBURNE-HANHAM, JP, 1915 - 1919
THE RIGHT HON. The EARL of SHAFTESBURY, KP, PC, GCVO, 1919 - 1922, 1924 - 1925
CAPTAIN THE RIGHT HON. F. E. GUEST, CBE, DSO, 1922 - 1924
CAPTAIN ANGUS V. HAMBRO, DL, JP, 1925-33, 1936 - 1944
LIEUT.-COL. SIR PHILIP COLFOX, BART, MC, 1933 - 1936
H.E. THE RIGHT HON. LORD LLEWELLIN, CBE, MC, TD, DL, 1944 - 1957
BRIGADIER G. M. B. FORTMAN, CB, TD, DL, 1957 - 1961
ROBERT TOM WARREN, 1962 - 1963
COLONEL SIR RICHARD GLYN, BART, OBE, TD, DL, 1964 - 1969
SIMON WINGFIELD DIGBY, MA, TD, DL, 1970 - 1984
SIR ANTHONY JOLLIFFE, GBE, DL, D.Sc, D.Mus, 1984 - 2011

Past Hon. Secretaries:
WILLIAM WATKINS, JP, 1904 - 1925
H. LL. WATKINS, 1925 - 1937
S. H. J. DUNN, 1937 - 1940
E. G. GALE, 1940 - 1941
HARRY J. HARVEY, 1941 - 1942
F. C. H. DENNETT, AACCA, FRES, 1942 - 1961
W. T. G. PERROTT, MIWO, 1961 - 1969
J. C. R. PREWER, 1969 - 1979
G. E. HINE, FRICS, 1979 - 2004

Past Hon. Editors:
SIR NEWMAN FLOWER, 1914 - 1920
STANLEY L. GALPIN, 1920 - 1932
H. LL. WATKINS, 1935 - 1937
ASHLEY C. ROGERS, 1937 - 1950
FRANK C. H. DENNETT, 1951 - 1960
N. J. ('NAT') BYLES, 1961 - 1978
FRED LANGFORD, 1979 - 1994
GEORGE LANNING, 1995 - 2000
PETER PITMAN, 2001 - 2013
TREVOR VACHER-DEAN, 2014 - 2015
SELWYN WILLIAMS, 2016 – 2019

INDEX *(Advertisers in Italics)*

YEAR BOOK CONTACTS

Editorial "The Dorset Year Book": Nicholas Wright
39 Cross Road, Weymouth, DT4 9QX. Tel 01305 459268
Email: wright1941@btinternet.com

Advertising: Stuart Adam
Court Barton, West Bagber, Taunton, Somerset TA4 3EQ
Tel: 01823 432076 Email: stu.adam@outlook.com

Sales & Distribution:
Position currently vacant but telephone
01305 833700

*When emailing in the first instance please also give your postal address.
Please also be patient – as volunteers we are not always "on call"
but we pledge to respond as quickly as possible.*

PRODUCTS PRINTED IN DORSET
USING SUSTAINABLE RESOURCES
AND THE LATEST TECHNOLOGY
print team
Est. 1991
www.printteam.co.uk

Thomas Fowell Buxton, MP for Weymouth and Melcombe Regis, 1818-1837.

Joyce Fannon

Thomas Fowell Buxton was not a Dorsetshire man born and bred. He was born at Castle Hedingham, Essex, in 1786 and baptised into the Church of England at St Nicholas Church. The family house at Earl's Colne, Colne House/Place, was bought a year later in 1787. The 5 children were brought up there until Anna Buxton, widowed in 1792, re-married in 1806 to banker Edmund Henning and moved to live in Weymouth, Dorset. It was said of young Buxton in Essex that "He was never a child; he was a man when in petticoats" and also that "He was a bold and determined character". For Buxton life at home at Earl's Colne had little indulgence but much liberty. [1]

In his early years, Thomas Fowell Buxton was sent to school in Kingston aged four and a half. His health deteriorated through ill-treatment at the school, so in the year of his father's death he was transferred to Dr Charles Burney's School at Greenwich. Being tall he earned the nickname, "Elephant Buxton". He reached 6' 4" as an adult, the same height as Abraham Lincoln. His headmaster said of him that he was the greatest reader of books in the school but all of them were trash.

Buxton left the Greenwich school aged 15 and was at home for a while before going to Ireland aged 16 years to be tutored for entry to Trinity College, Dublin. He distinguished himself at University to the extent that they asked him to represent the University in Parliament; a request he refused. After graduating, Buxton married Hannah Gurney in 1807. She was from an important Norfolk Quaker banking family. One of his sister-in-laws was Elizabeth Fry.

Buxton and his new wife were staying on Grandmother Sarah Buxton's estate at Belfield, Wyke Regis when the offer came of a job from a maternal Hanbury uncle. On entering the brewing firm of Truman and Hanbury, at a salary of £300 per year, he and his wife went to live in Spitalfields, in Brick Lane, London, near to the Black Eagle Brewery. One of the first things Buxton did at the brewery was to engage a teacher, so that the workers could learn to read and write. In 1810 he joined the board of management of The Society for Promoting the Royal British or Lancastrian System for the Education of the Poor. The following year he became a partner in the firm, Truman, Hanbury and Buxton.

On the death of his grandmother, Sarah Buxton, in 1814, he inherited Belfield House, Weymouth, Dorset, and let it with its 13 acres to his Uncle Charles Buxton. The family house at Earls Colne, Essex, had been "parted with" before 1810. As a property owner Buxton could vote and could potentially enter Parliament. On his numerous visits to Weymouth Buxton stayed at Belfield.

Belfield House as it stands today.
Photo reproduced by kind permission of John Stark & Crickmay Partnership, Architects, Dorchester

In 1816 he came to the notice of William Wilberforce, when Buxton made a speech at the Mansion House in support of the poor of London, especially the silk weavers of Spitalfields. They were feeling the effects of competition from cheap silk imports and from alternative textile industries in the newer industrialised towns of the north. The speech was published and £43,000 was raised; the Prince of Wales gave £5000. Wilberforce wrote to Buxton that he hoped he would enter, "an assembly in which I trust we shall be fellow-labourers". [2]

In 1818 Buxton wrote a book An Inquiry into Prison Discipline. It was translated into French. His father had been interested in prisons and the well-being of prisoners when High Sheriff of Essex and Buxton had visited Newgate Prison in the company of his sister-in-law, Elizabeth Fry and others. Later that year he was elected as MP for Weymouth and Melcombe Regis in Dorset; a position he was to hold for 19 years, standing in 8 riotous elections. In 1818 he wrote to his wife; "I wish you were here to see me chaired. The town is in an uproar. The bugle horn is at this moment playing, and hundreds of persons are collected on the Esplanade". [3]

He entered Parliament to promote prison reform and criminal law reform; there were 230 crimes for which the punishment could be hanging. In 1819 he spoke in Parliament about the appalling conditions on the "Hellships" taking prisoners from prison hulks to Australia. He and other MP's sat on Select Committees for Criminal Law and Prison Reform. These committees laid the groundwork for Sir Robert Peel's reforms of the 1820s. From these the Metropolitan Police would be formed and capital crimes were reduced from 230 to 8. Buxton had urged the ending of capital punishment except for murder: "to inflict death needlessly can be called by no other name than that of 'legal murder". [4] Until an alternate punishment could be sought he supported transportation.

In 1821 Wilberforce asked Buxton to take over from him in leading the Abolitionist MPs in Parliament. The Slave Trade had been abolished in 1807 but slavery still existed as an economic system; babies were born into slavery. Buxton took 18 months before agreeing. Perhaps Wilberforce saw the same qualities in Buxton as he himself possessed. Both were Evangelical Anglicans, though Buxton had joined Quakerism in 1807. He was disowned in 1817. He had been attending the services of an evangelical Anglican preacher, Rev Josiah Pratt and returned to the Anglican fold. Buxton still regarded himself as being half a Quaker. Most politicians had expected that Henry Brougham would be Wilberforce's successor not Buxton. Brougham was disappointed.

In 1821 Buxton sat on the Suttee Committee aiming to abolish the practice of burning widows alive on the funeral pyres of their Indian husbands. The hope was that suttee could be abolished through Parliament but it could be done only through India House; headquarters of the powerful East India Company. In 1827 Buxton wrote to and visited William Bentinck, recently appointed Governor General of India, urging him to ban the practice. One of the first things Bentinck did on reaching India was to ban suttee.

Buxton visited Weymouth twice in 1828. On his first visit in August he found his mother, Anna Henning, in good health. Later in the year he was back again to bury her at the Old Quaker Cemetery, Bridport. She had died at his older sister's home at Bradpole. His sister Anna, like her mother, had been Quaker. She had married William Forster and both were prominent members of the local Quaker community for over twenty years.

In 1829 much parliamentary business was taken up with The Catholic Question. Buxton was to vote for Catholic Emancipation against the will of his electors. He risked non-election next time round but voted with his conscience, for the good of Ireland. He always voted with his conscience, as he regarded himself as an Independent in Parliament and did not seek ministerial appointment, which would mean a commitment to a party. "My line is distinctly drawn. I care little about party politics. I vote as I like." [5] As time went on he would increasingly align with the reform Whig party

In the 1820s and 30s he championed the rights of free indigenous peoples in the Empire. The Khoi (Hottentots) and Xhosa (Caffre) in South Africa benefited from his interventions in Parliament, as did the Kaurna in the new colony of South Australia in 1836. In 1837 a street in Adelaide, the capital of the new colony, was named for him; his first recognition.

Back to slavery: By 1833 Buxton and the other abolitionist MPs succeeded in securing a Bill to abolish slavery throughout the British Empire. Before the debate on the Bill, Buxton asked for help in bringing in 187,000 petitions from the women of Great Britain. Three MPs were needed to carry them in. It was a moment of theatre with cat-calls from the opposition and cheers for supporters of the Bill. The Bill included £20,000,000 compensation for people who had investments in slavery and a 12 year apprenticeship system. Buxton entered an amendment for the latter to be reduced to 1 year. It was defeated but the final Bill included a reduced apprenticeship system to end in 1840 for field slaves and a shorter one for domestics to end in 1838. The only ones fully free were children under 6. Many abolitionists considered that Buxton should have voted against the Bill because of its imperfections, but he felt that this was an opportunity for abolition that might not present itself again. The Act for the Abolition of Slavery throughout the British Empire excluded the possessions of the East India Company (India and St Helena) and the Crown Colony of Ceylon. The Act came into effect the following year on 1st August 1834; it was a proud moment. The family termed him "The Liberator".

Buxton was also to be proud of having chaired the Aborigenes Committee in 1836. The term "Aborigenes" then covered all indigenous peoples. The Committee reported the following year and, its provisions, being adopted as policy by the Colonial Office, secured the rights of indigenous peoples throughout the burgeoning Empire. Sadly later generations were to ignore its principles.

In 1837 William IV died and Victoria became Queen. A General Election was called. Buxton set out his priorities for his future actions in Parliament. Amongst them he was aiming for the global abolition of the slave trade. Brazil and Cuba still traded extensively in slaves. Also, included was his concern for the treatment of indentured labour being brought in legally to replace former slave-labour. The source of much of this indentured labour supply was the Indian sub-continent.

Disappointingly at the election of 1837 Buxton was not returned to Parliament. 27 constituencies asked for him to stand for them, but he decided to retire from politics. So he was in the Visitors' Gallery next year, 1838, when the apprenticeship system was over-turned. He and his party were so jubilant that they were asked to leave for riotous behaviour.

"Buxton's Memorial Statue in Westminster Abbey" Copyright Dean & Chapter of Westminster.

In 1840 he was made a Baronet of "Belfield in the County of Dorset and Runton in the County of Norfolk", in recognition of his work in Parliament. His motto was from Ecclesiastes: "Whatever they hand findeth to do, do it with thy might". Stephen Farrell, in his article on the Parliamentary website, says that Buxton's career as MP for Weymouth and Melcombe Regis, "Was held up as a model of religious and philanthropic excellence".[6]

1845 Sir Thomas Fowell Buxton died at his home, Northrepps, in Norfolk, aged 57. Prince Albert set up a fund to erect a statue in Buxton's memory in Westminster Abbey. The statue cost £1,500 and £450 of this was given by ex-slaves in Sierra Leone, South Africa and the Caribbean. The Buxton statue stands in the North Aisle of the Abbey near to the statue of his mentor, William Wilberforce.

So Buxton is remembered by the statue in Westminster Abbey and the Buxton Fountain in Victoria Tower Gardens, Westminster. Other memorials comprise the Buxton Tower at the Mico University College in Jamaica, a plaque in Norwich Cathedral and the street named after him in Adelaide, South Australia. In Africa there is a bust of him in St George's Cathedral in Freetown, Sierra Leone. Two villages are named after him, the Buxton village near Georgetown, Guyana and the village of Buxton in Ontario Canada.

Thanks to the efforts of the Thomas Fowell Buxton Society, the Buxton Monument was erected on Bincleaves Green, Weymouth, in 2017. It is recognition from the town that he represented in Parliament for 19 years. It was designed by a student, Peter Loizou, at Weymouth College Masonry Department and comprises 144 stones hand-carved by fellow students. The hand-carved stones were part of the practical assessment for gaining the Level 2 Diploma in stone masonry. The students benefited; Buxton as educationalist would have approved.

Epitaph by a friend: "His sympathy was awakened by men he had never seen, and he gave the best years of his life to their welfare" (Rev J W Cunningham). [7]

[1] Charles Buxton, *Memoirs of Sir Thomas Fowell Buxton,* (London: John Murray, 1850), p 2.

[2] Buxton, *Memoirs of Sir Thomas Fowell Buxton,* p 52.

[3] Buxton, *Memoirs of Sir Thomas Fowell Buxton,* p 67.

[4] Oliver Barclay, *Thomas Fowell Buxton and the Liberation of Slaves* (York: William Sessions Ltd, 2001), p 49

[5] Barclay *Thomas Fowell Buxton and the Liberation of slaves,* p 45.

[6] *www.parliament.uk*

[7] Buxton, *Memoirs of Sir Thomas Fowell Buxton,* p 505.

Biography - Joyce Fannon BA MA PGCE

Joyce was a co-founder of the Thomas Fowell Buxton Society in Weymouth in 2010. As Society education officer, she has given numerous presentations on behalf of the Society. These have been mainly in Dorset, though in 2018 she gave one in Castle Hedingham, Essex, Buxton's birthplace. In the same year she gave a presentation at Portcullis House, Westminster to an audience that included parliamentarians. This was to celebrate the 200th anniversary of the election to Parliament of Thomas Fowell Buxton as MP for Weymouth and Melcombe Regis. With the erection of the Buxton Monument on Bincleaves Green, Weymouth in 2017, the Society produced a book *A Monumental Endeavour*. It comprises 11 articles giving details on various aspects of Buxton's life, the Society and the Monument. This can be purchased online at www.thomasfowellbuxton.org.uk , where more information about the Society can be accessed.

Arringe Juice an Moosli

By Sue Worth

(An old Dorset farmer who has worked the land all his life hands down advice to a youngster just out of agricultural college. Ed.)

Caw, you'm lookin fair shrammed my Son
- Git down off thick tracter.

Jump up an down an flap yer arms about
fer a bit. That's right - You'm all soft you
chaps frum town. You aint got the first idea
ow to keep yerselves warm

Now -
What might you ave ad fer breakfast s'marnin?
Arringe Juice an Moosli !
Now there's a meal fer a workin man,
Arringe Juice an Moosli.

- Course I seed 'Moosli' afore.
Looks like the sweepins off the granary floor if you ask me

Thick wife a yourn'll kill thee wi all this ealthy eatin
Arringe Juice an Moosli!

You want a breakfast as'll keep ee warm
Parridge, or I favour a girt pan a chiltlins an
pork sausages, nicely fried, along wi a andfull
a field mushrooms. Bread and two or three
fresh eggs. All washed down wi a girt mug a tea,
wi six or seven spoonfulls a sugar in ee

A good wold coat wudden go amiss,
an zomat to cover thee silly ead – though
there's nothin useful inside

A layer a goose grease smeared on the chest
Is certain to keep out cold - A layer a
goose grease an a warm woolly vest

Smell! Don't you worry about smell my son.
She'll put up wi a bit a smell if she do love ee

I don't old wi all this washin meeself - Taint ealthy.
Saps a mans strength, only dirty people need cleanin

Just you think yerself lucky you didn't
work the land when I were a lad.
Hedgin and ditchin can wreak havoc wi a man

Still, it was done religious in them days
be craftsmen who knew what they were at.
Not be some girt fool of a machine slashin away regardless

Fair breaks my eart it do, seein the mess they do make of it

- Just what I was tellin im this very minute Maister

"You git back up on thick tracter I zaid "You aint paid to stand
about ere lookin useless" You cain't trust these college chaps out
of your sight. Scive off soon as look at ee they will – not like us wold uns

Still, you cain't really blame im – You'll never guess
what is Mrs give im fer brekfast s'marnin
Arringe Juice an Moosli – I ask thee

Arringe Juice an Moosli!

"Who Is It?" "It's the Postman"

Memories of Geoffrey Pritchard – a 1960s Christmas postman

Geoffrey Pritchard

The wind scattered any leaves left in Barrack Road, Weymouth as I walked through the entrance into the parade ground of the Red Barracks, then being used as a sorting office for the G.P.O. It was 7.15 a.m. on 17 December 1965, and I was reporting for duty as a Christmas postman.

I had completed an application form about a month previously and, having heard nothing, assumed that it was unsuccessful. As I arrived home late the previous evening, my father gave me the news that I had a job. The fact that the start time was at an early hour which like most teenagers "I didn't do" was sweetened by his offer of a lift.

My fellow posties were a mixed bunch - sixth formers like myself, university students, some teachers (taking advantage of the school holidays starting early) and some who described themselves as students, but to my 17 year old eyes seemed middle-aged.

I was greeted cheerfully by the full- time posties, many of whom were middle aged ex- servicemen. It was their task to sort the mail, mine to deliver. I heaved a fully laden bag across my shoulders. "Ere, young'un. If you get peckish, thic shop down 'ope Cove do sell very good baasties!", my postman mentor called out helpfully at my retreating form.

My round, which consisted of two deliveries per day, was part of Chapelhay, conveniently only a short distance from the sorting office. This was an area of Victorian terraces, and an inner core which had, only 25 years previously, been devastated by bombing and memories of some of the older residents were still very clear.

I had a few preconceptions about the role. Stories abounded about postmen being chased by dogs and fingers bitten when one pushed the letters through the letterbox. One story which stuck in my mind was told by a classmate whose father, a decorated Royal Naval C.P.O. had joined the postal service on his retirement. He was out on his deliveries and paused to remove the mail from his bundle. As he pushed the post through the letterbox of one house he glanced up to see through the large opaque glass pane, the voluptuous form a woman, stark naked, coming down the hall. Seeing him she let out a shriek and disappeared. Fortunately - or perhaps unfortunately I did not suffer a similar experience.

Some of the street names were confusing, as there were terraces which had at some time been renamed. An envelope with the name "Pansy Terrace" in a spidery hand caused some initial puzzlement, but I soon realised that it had been renamed Prospect Terrace some time in the past. Newberry Road was another cause of confusion, as until only recently opposite sides had been called Newberry Terrace and Dorset Place respectively, until the whole street had been redesignated Newberry Road. This must have been even more confusing before the Second World War, as there was

another street a couple of hundred yards away named Dorset Terrace!
Chapelhay in those days appeared to be a trusting community. I trudged up the flight of stairs to the first floor of Chapelhay Heights to find a note pinned to an open door "Just gone over Gordon Row shops. Back in 10 mins." This was before the days of security doors, entry phones and keypads.

The amount some people tried to cram into an envelope astonished me. I spent some mornings trying to reunite the photographs of someone's grandchildren which had burst from their envelopes with the accompanying letters. I soon became a minor authority on handwriting as it happened at least six times during the week. I was not so lucky in my attempts to deliver a Christmas pudding as the letterbox dated from the Victorian era and the householder was never in. Whether the regular post Christmas postman had better luck I do not know. I hope he did not beat my eleven attempts.

Some houses revealed surprises. I remember calling at one terraced house for the door to be opened after a long pause by a tall, gaunt man whom I used to see riding an elderly tradesman's bicycle round the town, often carrying scrap iron in the basket. The hall was piled high with scrap – including at least two domestic hot water cylinders. I assumed that he lived there on his own, as he could barely squeeze past to open the door.

I had only two dog experiences. One, in Franchise Street, was between me and an unknown canine. Every morning as I stuffed the post through the letterbox there was a growl, a sound of running feet and a crash as the door shook when something I imagined to resemble the Hound of the Baskervilles collided with it.

The other was of a more comical nature. One property on the ground floor in Chapelhay Heights fronting Dorset Terrace had a front door directly to the outside world. Even though it was in the depths of winter, the front door was left open. On my first morning there was a yapping and growling and a Pekingese ran towards me from the back of the hall. I put the letters hurriedly on the floor and made my exit. The next morning there were similar noises from the far end of the hall. I put the post on the ground and smartly stepped aside. The Pekingese appeared at my waist level, then I realised that it was on an elasticated lead. About two feet outside the property it was suddenly catapulted backwards as the full stretch of the elastic was reached. I glimpsed an expression of astonishment come over its face and it landed with a loud thump and yelp at the far end of the hall.

I certainly learned a lot about the neighbourhood and its residents. Friendly old ladies who, on reflection, might not have had any other visitors stopped for a chat when I rang the bell. Some were surprisingly athletic when they discovered that some of the post, although it bore their address, was not for them. The rule was "If it has that address it has to go through the letterbox." I explained this to one elderly man as he pursued me up the lower part of Franchise Street on a dark morning clad in his dressing gown.

Too soon my time came to an end, but it left me with an appreciation of the work postmen do, so often overlooked by many. Incidentally, I never did get to the pasty shop!

Varmer John

By Hayne Russell

If anything went wrong in the village it was always "Varmer John" who was sent for to deal with it. One time it was on account of an old man in the village who had been taken ill with delirium tremens. He was a big strong fellow, twice the size of "Varmer John" and vowing murder to anyone who came near him. However, John pinned down his arms and held him till all the " blue devils" had disappeared.

Another time a workman got himself trapped in a foul well and a volunteer was asked for to go down. "Varmer John" went down and pulled him back up putting his own life at risk. However, it was when he shot the mad dog that he became immortal although it was meant to be kept as a secret.

It was the middle of the night and John was asleep when came a thunderous knock on his door. It was repeated until he put his head out of the window.
"'Tis on'y I" came a voice. "There be a mad dog about, mad as ee' kin be" "Will 'ee come out 'n shoot 'n?"

"But I've never handled a gun in my life" said John "Only at the fair"

"Niver mind be that" the voice answered "If thee don' shoot ' n vust time, these kin try agin"

His eyes becoming accustomed to the darkness he saw the dim outline of a man with a gun over his shoulder.

"Can't you shoot" said John

"Aye, but I be aveard I'll miss 'n. Do 'ee cum quick zur. Zee tis maester's gun an' 'ee told I t' cum an' ask 'ee t' shoot 'n"

Thinking that further delay could be dangerous John flung on some clothes ran downstairs and took the gun from the agitated man who still stood gazing at the window, as if he thought that was where aid would come.

"Now then where is this animal ?" commanded John who was by now fully awake, the sense of danger quickening his senses. But even as he spoke he heard a frenzied bark and the creature came careering madly toward him.

"Stand still man" he shouted

The dog tore past them and steadily John took aim. There was a sharp report and then silence. They walked a few yards down the road and there by the roadside lay the poor creature its suffering over. The bullet had struck it in the head and it lay with its tongue out, its last desire having been to slake its terrible thirst at the river which lay at the end of the road.

"He's dead zur, dead be a door nail" said the man.

"Isn't that what you wanted"? enquired John

"Yes zur but 'ee were a beautiful creature avore this madness took 'en. 'Ee wudden 'urt nar man. 'oman nor child. But thank 'ee zur" he added "You be a game young veller I don't wonder maidens won't be atter 'ee. Will 'ee promise. zur that thee won't zay nothin' 'bout this yer business ?"

"Well yes, if you wish it" grinned "Varmer John"

"Thank 'ee kindly zur. I'm much obliged to 'ee. Zee I kin tell maister 'twere I as zhot 'n. an' perhaps 'ee might raise me wages" !

Terms of Description and Abuse in Dorset

By Hilary Townsend

"That door do plim. T'is the rain do make en plim".
This word `plim` is a word that was heard regularly in my North Dorset childhood and it meant that the rain had caused the door to swell. It was a good old Dorset vernacular term but I never seem to hear it now.

When I was a child before the war I can remember Mrs Cluett who lived on Church Hill, Stalbridge, looking out across towards Stourton Tower at an approaching storm of rain and saying
`Why, the sky is as black as the Devil`s nutting bag`.

And Mrs Prout who lived in Westminster Cottages remarked of someone who had no conversation and whom she found very dull:
`She's not hard of hearing` She said `She's as deaf as an adder`.

Nellie Titterington,who helped me look after my mother in the old age of them both, was a parlour maid at Max Gate for the Hardys and then went on to work for, as she put it, the `real gentry`. She told me when she was running the household of the widower there:
`When I did need a nikky for the drawing room fire, the underservants had get it at once`. A nikky she told me was a small faggot of wood.

`A `vooty` thing, William Barnes explained, was a small useless object. And a `stunpoll` he also defined as a blockhead or a tree that was almost dead.

`Athirt` meaning `across` or `over` was a word I loved as a child when my father used to tell me that the wood pigeon's song as he built his careless nest, ran:

`Two sticks across and one athirt and that will doooco`

But he explained, the only bit of the song you ever heard was `dooooo`.

As well as terms of description, there were terms of abuse I heard in my childhood that we never seem to hear now. What did we say when we were annoyed with someone or despised them in those far-off days - days which I seem to remember ever more clearly now? We had a good range of terms.

If someone gave themselves airs above what Stalbridge perceived to be their station in life they were described as `bigetty`. I'm not quite sure how you spell bigetty, but it seemed to me pretty graphic at the time. A skinny undernourished person was `a scarecrow` while a thick person or a child who was not very bright was described as `a doughbake`. Mr Trewhella, the headmaster of the Senior School, the one at the top of Church Hill which is now a private house, would sometimes use it in relation to a child or children.

`You doughbake` He would exclaim, rolling the word round his tongue and explaining that it must be a peculiarly North Dorset term because he had never heard it in his native Cornwall.

`Fathead` was a term used not so much to describe the thick as someone who got the wrong end of the stick or got a simple task wrong.

People in Stalbridge, who thought themselves much better than their neighbours and were so unwise as to let their opinion show, were described as `stuck up`. A Mother's darling, or any young man who could not face up to the rigours of country life, was described as `a milk sop` while some-one whose constitution was on the soft side was described as `nesh`. I have heard my father, torment-ed by wind burn in the evening after a day spent outdoors in a high wind, observe that the trouble was his skin had always been `nesh`.

When in the early 1950s I went to work in London I took with me various Dorset dialect words but had no idea that they were local dialect words. until somebody asked what I meant or laughed at what I said. I used the word `ground` as Dorset people do, sounding it out richly as grou-wwnnnd and when I described Hampstead Heath is a wonderful stretch of open grouwwnnnd I got a round of laughter.

One day, looking through the window of my office, high up in a busy road just off Oxford Street during a storm, I said:

`Oh look, the water's coming through the `shuting` meaning that the water was running down and leaking from what Londoners called a gutter on the edge of the roof. Now to me a gutter was the thing that was installed in every cow stall, , so it took a few minutes to sort that out. I soon got used to being laughed at but I think, looking back, it made me more determined to hang onto my lovely old Dorset words. Now though, well into the 21st century, will it be possible to keep any of them much longer?

Me, I know how I have always been and still am described, with my face as round as the Stilton cheese, I'm a real `Dorset Dumpling`!

Memories of Growing Up In Dorchester

(The late John White was born in Dorchester in 1931 and died in New Zealand in 2017. He was a long serving overseas member and over the years he sent many articles to the Year Book. This article was from his memoirs and the one that follows – "My Dad An Unsung Hero" was found in his effects. Christabel Rimmer, John's long-term partner in New Zealand, has sent them in for publication. We are grateful to Christabel. Ed.)

Dorchester, set in the heart of the rolling hills and valleys of Dorset, was a wonderful playground to grow up in. A small town full of historic buildings, and flanked on three sides by the Walks of the old Roman walls, an easy town to walk around. The nearby woods and streams were a superb adventure ground for growing boys.

My brother George and I loved tobogganing down Maumbury Rings, the old Roman earth amphitheatre on the outskirts of town. We also often played in the Borough gardens just down from the back of our home at the end of Bowling Alley Walk. Further afield was Maiden Castle, a solitary hill fort, the triple earth ramparts of which rise 60 feet high - a fascination to me even today. What a wealth of history lies there, and we relished an opportunity to walk on those impressive earthen ramparts. We both had catapults and bows and arrows and there were plenty of places to play Cowboys and Indians – and even Romans and Ancient Britons, often with neighbouring boys, but as George was four years older than me, inevitably as he grew older he played with a different set of friends. The river was also a favourite playing ground. I can remember my school friends and I trying to catch fish, as well as other rough and tumble games that sometimes threatened to end in the water.

There were extensive riverside walks of considerable beauty, and as a family, on a Sunday after church if the weather allowed, we would go for a stroll along the banks of the River Frome. A most impressive river stroll ran just to the North of the town with a rather longer, more strenuous walk to the South. This took us through Came Woods and onto Came Golf Course in an area called Ridgeway. When I was very young I recall my father killing an Adder with his walking stick on Came Golf Course. I was quite a young child and in a pushchair when this happened, so it is a very early childhood memory. From Ridgeway one could look to the South for a magnificent view of Weymouth Bay and on the odd occasion we would walk the eight or nine miles from Dorchester through Preston to Weymouth and then catch the train back to Dorchester.

If it was wet on a Sunday afternoon, the dining table would be folded away and the track of our Hornby 'O' gauge railway came into use. It was the start of a lifelong love of trains – especially steam. I was often to be found at the Railway Yards looking for rides in the cabs of the steam engines. Dorchester South Station had a very unusual layout. Passenger trains were obliged to carry out complicated and bizarre manoeuvres which never ceased to fascinate me, I spent hours watching the manoeuvres and became quite an expert on engines and steam trains; a hobby that lasted a lifetime.

Often I'd visit my grandmother's in Bridport. She ran the Ship Inn and owned a black curly haired retriever who combined sociability with the regulars during opening hours with a true guard dog's behaviour after closing time. Curly and I were great friends and on visits to Bridport I'd take him for walks. He was a fantastic swimmer and I recall walking him on a lead on West Bay Beach with strict instructions not to let him go into the water, but Curly had a mind of his own and wanted a swim. I hung on like grim death to the last, trying to keep him from the water, but I too ended up taking a swim as he dragged me in with him.

Both my parents were good Church of England people and we knelt at prayer by the bed every night. We also went to C of E Sunday School. Although I started out my schooling at a Church of England school, at the age of six I was transferred to the local Catholic school. This was after an incident where I suffered a broken arm. My teacher had ignored my pain and I endured it for the rest of the day, but the break was apparent to my parents when I arrived home and, as far as my mother was concerned, the teacher was guilty of gross negligence. I will never know what was said to the Principal but I was transferred to the St Mary's Catholic school to complete my primary education, and later in 1942, I went on to Dorchester Grammar School.

The war years held a special fascination. There was a huge build up of American Military. personnel in Dorchester. Some were housed at the local Barracks when they first arrived in 1943, but most went to Poundbury, which was an Army camp at that time. The Americans were a great fascination to the boys of Dorchester (and probably the girls as well, although as a 12 year old I was too young to register that). I made friends with a couple of Americans and they would sometimes come to dinner with my family. We lived in very modest, cramped quarter above our shoe shop but they never seemed to mind, just enjoyed our homely hospitality, and often brought chocolate or some small thing from their stores. They disappeared after they sailed from Weymouth as part of the D-Day offensive. Ever since I've wondered how they fared.

German Prisoners of War were also camped in Dorchester. They were used as labourers and farm hands, and I can recall seeing them marching through the centre of town going too and from their work.
My friends and I often played at war games and sometimes made make-shift bombs which had the potential to cause damage; on one occasion we actually burnt out the middle of a huge bush in my friend's garden - something to which we never owned up of course, but watched with guilty amusement as, months later, the adults tried to work out how it had died.

I remember a day in 1940, watching 40 Heinkel Luftwaffe bombers flying menacingly overhead accompanied by a large fighter escort. I was watching Mum play bowls at the time, and everyone stopped and looked up. It was very scary but so fascinating I was rooted to the spot. There were many such incidents which were scary and exciting at the same time. Dorchester was never the direct target of the German bombers but often we could see the glow in the sky at night time, caused by the burning towns in the distance that had been bombed. And often the siren would sound the alert and we'd spend the night in the air-raid shelter. Dorchester was blessed with a few public air raid shelters built of brick and reinforced concrete, and a shelter for 100 people was built in Bowling Alley Walk immediately at our back door. It had two chemical toilets - the very latest in modernity. In the interests of public morality (no sex please) they were kept locked, only to be unlocked when the enemy were to hand. Our good churchgoing family held the key as at least one of us was always on hand, either in the shop or the flat above. At first, when the Luftwaffe were overhead, we always went to the air raid shelter immediately the siren sounded, but as the winter of 1940-41 progressed we became a little more brave and stayed in bed as long as we felt it safe. It was also our job to carry a flask of tea and an emergency first aid kit into the shelter, (to be used only if the anti aircraft guns in the immediate vicinity started to fire). Once we got used to the raids I think we kept a nice balance between preserving the public morality by keeping the shelter locked, and preserving the public from the Luftwaffe by opening it just in time.

I well remember freezing nights trying to sleep on the hard wooden benches of the shelter as the Luftwaffe streamed overhead to Bristol, Bath, Cardiff and the industrial cities of the Midlands and the North. One night I awoke in absolute panic, worse than any sirens or the drone of enemy aircraft overhead ever induced. The cause was a schoolboy prank - Ken Satchel (the little devil) had dropped a black beetle into my ear as I slept.

When the fireworks for the night finished we gratefully crept back into our homes exhausted. The precious key – that guardian of the public morals – also returned to its resting place ready to unlock the shelter again the next time danger threatened, which it sometimes did five or six times a day.

Curly, my Grandmother's dog was a source of great fun when the air raid siren sounded. It was an additional reason for enjoying a visit to Bridport during the war years, and it also kept the pub patrons amused. Dogs, as you are aware, have a greater hearing range than we humans, and we always had advanced warning of the siren from Curly who would howl almost a perfect imitation of the siren's wail fully 10 seconds before it was audible to the human ear. This happened whether the siren sounded the "warning" or the "all clear" signal. He was truly a great character of a dog.

Ration books and gas masks became part of everyday life. We had to carry the gas masks with us and we practised wearing them both at home and at school. We got used to food shortages and I remember becoming very angry after standing in a queue for a rare cake sale, after a woman pushed into the line a short way in front of me on spying someone she knew. The cake ran out just as I reached the front and I was so irate, and disappointed that none of the adults had complained about someone pushing in, that I'm sure it was a formative moment in my development. I became an embryo socialist, perhaps somewhat idealistically, and unquestionably believed from that day onwards in "fair shares for all".

Dorchester Grammar School ran a Cadet training scheme and I joined the Junior Training Corps. I still possess the book given to me as a prize for Meritorious Service as an NCO in my final years – definitely designed to rid a boy of any glamorous notions he might have about war; the title, "For Whom The Bell Tolls" by Ernest Hemingway.

My Childhood, like the war, was over by then; I was 17, and a year later I left school to do my National Service. My visits to Dorchester were brief intervals after that; firstly on leave from the Army, then between terms at Oxford University. After University I taught at Clifton College, Bristol, for a couple of years, then went overseas to Kenya and Tanzania, and later to Australia and New Zealand, but I have remained at heart a Dorset boy.

My Dad - An Unsung Hero

by John White

My father, William George White, was born and bred in Dorchester, and apart from active service in the First World War, when he was posted to India then Mesopotamia (present day Iraq), he lived in Dorchester all his life. He owned the shoe shop that fronted the Great Western Road and I grew up in the cramped flat above it.

It was now 1965; I was 33 and had been in Sydney only a few months when my brother phoned to say that Dad had suffered a heart attack and the outlook was bad. I quickly made arrangements to get to Dorchester but dad died on April 30th before my plane took off.

The funeral was held a couple of days after I arrived in Dorchester and afterwards friends and family gathered at my brothers house. I knew very few of Dad's friends having left home at 18, immediately after finishing school, but a few of Dad's old comrades from the 4th Battalion were there and I was introduced to Windy Gale, who had been in the army with Dad – his Company Sergeant Major in fact.

Dad had been a short man, barely reaching my chin, and I was surprised to find that Windy was shorter still. Surprised, because I had been in the Guards and it was usual for a Sergeant Major in the Guards to be at least six foot tall. Many were three or four inches taller than that. Windy must have been 70 or so, alert and beady eyed with not an ounce of fat on his miniature frame. He reminded me of a small lightweight boxing champion. He had a youthful confident voice, thick grey hair cut in a Sergeant Major's haircut – short back and sides – and a Sergeant Major's demeanour if ever I saw one.

"So you're John" he said. "Your dad often talked about you when I called into the shop. He was always very proud of you, and I think he said you were a Sergeant in the Guards regiment?"

His alert eagle eye was on me. Regardless of his short stature he had a naturally commanding presence and in spite of the informal occasion I unconsciously reacted by standing ram-rod erect, shoulders back and stomach in. I had to make a conscious effort not to call him 'Sir' when I replied, "Yes, that's right".

"A paratrooper too, I seem to recall?"

I felt a little embarrassed at this old soldier talking about my Army history and added, "Yes, but I never saw active service. Unlike you and Dad I was never sent anywhere dangerous"

Smiling he replied "Well you'd never have got me jumping from a bloody plane". Changing the subject he said, "But let's talk about your dad. I could never understand why he'd never take a stripe. You know he absolutely refused promotion".

"I never knew that" I replied.

"Did he ever tell you about the Battle of Ramadi in Mespot ?" he asked.
"He mentioned it" I said, " but he never really told me what happened. I got the impression it was a bit of a shambles".
"It was a bit of a shambles all right! Johnny Turk gave us a right bloody hiding when we least expected it. We'd been chasing them over the desert for two or three days prior, so we thought the Battalion attack would be a walk-over. There was a gentle slope leading down to the Turkish position where they'd dug in – so now we were going to finish 'em off – artillery support and all that.

"There were three Rifle Companies leading the attack. Our Company –' B' Company – were the reserve company. We were strung out in one long line behind the other three, and we all expected the Turks would just make a little show of it and then throw in the towel. We'd made absolute mince meat of them in the couple of days we'd had them on the run. They'd suffered really heavy casualties as they retreated, whilst we'd suffered hardly any ourselves. However, now they put up a really heavy bombardment. A few minutes after the advance had started, the three forward companies were slowed - the Turks had a lot more artillery than we'd thought. They were good too; they hit what they fired at! The advance came to a halt, and with it our Company also came to a stop. We lay down, still in a single line behind the three forward companies, and were able to fire right over their heads at the Turks' trenches. We gave what support we could, but the Turks' artillery was bloody good and we could see our three forward companies were getting the worst of it. They were taking a terrible beating and it was obvious they'd bitten off more than they could chew, but they held on.

"After an hour or so the order was passed from man to man along our company line that we were to stand fast whilst the survivors of the other three companies retreated through our lines; our job was to give what support we could until they got over the ridge behind us and out of the direct fire of the Turks. The Turkish artillery followed their retreat as they started to come back through our line and 'B' Company got plastered too! It was hell!

"When the three companies were over the crest we poor beggars were on the hillside on our own, facing the Turks – just a long single line of us firing away. We were completely exposed as we weren't in trenches; each man just had a little wall of sand that he'd been able to shovel up in front of himself. Not enough to stop a bullet in most cases, and certainly no cover against the Turkish artillery. By now 'B' Company's casualties were mounting up and we were running short of ammunition. Believe it or not the word came, man to man along the line, that we could undo the two top buttons of our tunics!

"The word also came that when the whistle blew we were to scarper – run like hell up that bloody slope and take up position at the top of the crest. Our own artillery would do what they could to cover our retreat.

"The whistle went and it was every man for himself. The sun beat down like a furnace. Just to walk in the desert on a day like this was purgatory, but we had to run up that slope carrying a rifle and the rest of an infantryman's clobber. The Turkish artillery followed us as we ran – they killed a lot of men in 'B' Company that day.

"I got to the top and looked back down the hill and was amazed to see two of our blokes still there, right over on the left flank, firing away at the Turks; fighting their own little private war. I didn't realise at the time, but one of 'em was your Dad. What had happened was this: they were the last two blokes left alive on the left flank of the Company line. The four or five blokes immediately to their right had been killed, so the order to retreat never got to them. They were paying so much attention to the Turks in front of them that they never noticed the rest of the company getting the hell out of it; amongst the smoke and noise of the shelling they never even heard the whistle. It was quite a while before they realised what had happened – then they started to run!

They were just two men on that hillside, one big and one small, and the Turkish artillery shelled them. I watched horrified. I didn't think they had a chance. Then the big bloke fell – that was Lofty Wilson you know, the engine driver who retired a year or so ago. I'm sure you'd know him? (I did know Lofty; as a treat once when I was a kid he'd given me a ride in the cab of a steam engine whilst shunting in the West Yard).

"When Lofty went down your Dad stopped. Lofty was a big bloke but your Dad - not much bigger than me - stops and picks him up. He's carrying not just Lofty but Lofty's rifle and his own rifle too. He staggered up that hill with the whole Turkish Army firing at them. Then your Dad drops on one knee. I thought he'd been hit as well, but no – he'd stopped to pick up a bloody Lewis Gun! I don't know how he did it. There was this little bloke, staggering up the hill, carrying Lofty Wilson – a giant of a man – two rifles and a bloody Lewis gun! At the crest we were cheering them on and giving what covering fire we could. Finally your Dad collapsed over the crest of the hill without a scratch. Breathless, gasping for air fit to die he was. Lofty had the detonator tube of a bloody great shell sticking out in front, just under his collar bone and protruding out the back through his shoulder. Your Dad was dead beat but he hadn't got a scratch. All he wanted was water – "water, water", he kept saying.

"At the end of the day out of the one hundred who'd started off, there were only fourteen left fit to fight in the Company, including me and your Dad. We all wore those tall pith helmets – rather like a bobby's helmet. Short-ass as he was .. (Windy Gale's eyes glinted with humour as he grinned up at me towering above him) "... Short-ass as he was, a shell had taken the top clean off your Dad's helmet – and he wasn't even aware of it till I told him" Windy shook with laughter. "When I told him he nearly fainted. Your father really was lucky that day; by rights we should have buried him then, fifty years ago in 1917. If he'd been your height he would have had his bloody head taken off – and you wouldn't be here now young John!".

Windy was lost in reflection for a few minutes before he sighed saying, "I was only a Platoon Sergeant at that time but as all the officers were gone - the Company Sergeant Major and Colour Sergeant were gone too - I was left in command of what was left of 'B' Company. Anyway, I put your Dad in for a medal, but nothing ever came of it. I suppose because there was no commissioned officer to witness what had happened. Bloody pity – he deserved a gong for that, your father. And a pity he'd turned down promotion too. You could always rely on him and he would have made a great Platoon Sergeant Started in the Army as a Private and finished as a Private - I'll never understand why. He was a hero in my book".

Windy proffered his empty glass.

"By the way John, it's whisky I'm drinking"

"Yes, Sergeant Major, right away!". I marched off to get him a refill.

The Corfu Incident

Lieutenant Commander R. K. P. Abbott RNR (Retd)

Any of you who are ex Navy might well be aware of the 1946 Corfu Incident, and others won't, so let's have a look at the full facts.

Let us start with the date. It was 15th May 1946. That's more than a whole year after the end of the war in Europe.

On that day two Royal Navy warships were steaming south at a steady ten knots towards the island of Corfu. They were the cruisers HMS Orion and HMS Superb. On the port hand was the coast of Albania and ahead was the narrow channel to Corfu. When the ships were off the port of Saranda a shore battery started firing four-inch shells at them. Remember that we had just won WW2 and we had a massive navy of some 3000 ships at that time.

Rear Admiral Kinahan, who was flying his flag in Orion, ordered an increase in speed and the shots fell astern with no hits being made. On arrival at Corfu the admiral signalled to his CinC in Malta informing of the incident. However, it would be some eight days before the British public knew anything about this insult to our national pride and the reason for the suppression of this news has never been explained.

There was an exchange of diplomatic notes in which the Albaníans claimed that it had all been a mistake as they had not been able to identify the two ships. An outrageous statement as the ships were close inshore and were flying large White Ensigns ready for entering Corfu Harbour.

Let us now look at the state of the then Albania and consider why they had shelled. For more than 2000 years they had been occupied by foreign powers. First the Romans, then, in succession, Goths, Serbs, Greeks and Normans. And then, after 1400, they suffered 500 years under Turkish domination with the Moslem religion imposed with ferocity, cutting them off from historical and cultural ties with Europe.

They lost their own language and their culture was supressed. However, uprisings between 1909 and 1912 led to freedom from the Turks, and Albania was accepted by the European powers as an independent country. Sadly, this freedom was short lived. The outbreak of WW1 resulted in French, Italian and Serbian troops occupying regions of the country, declaring it a protectorate.

In 1920, following much wrangling, Italy withdrew and Albania became a member of the League of Nations. Ahmed Zogu was elected President in 1925 but, in 1928, in pursuance of grandiose ambitions, he declared himself King Zog the 1st, and ruled in tyranny, just like the Turks.

At this time a young Albanian student, named Enver Hoxha, emigrated to Paris where he studied Marxist-Leninist communism. Meanwhile the Italians increased their hold on the Country and signed a defensive alliance with Zog who subsequently filched monies from the State Treasury. Mussolini's troops invaded in 1939 and Zog fled, never to return.

After his studies in Paris Hoxha returned to run a tobacconist shop in Tirana but this was in fact the HQ of the National Communist Party. On the outbreak of WW2 the Germans entered Albania and Hoxha took to the mountains. He joined the partisans and became a successful leader, holding the rank of Colonel-General when the Germans left in 1944.

The communists were planning a revolution and Hoxha was the obvious choice as leader. In October 1944 he came to power and declared "The First Democratic Government of Albania". He ranted against "imperialists" who did not understand that Albania had won her freedom after 2000 years. He declined America's offer of Marshall Aid and he expelled all opponents, including old friends and even those who had fought with him as partisans. Now cut off from the Western Powers he was close to Tito and Stalin, and he went on to declare that he was prepared to defend Albania's borders by land or sea. Hence the shelling of our cruisers. But worse was yet to come, with "Murder in the Channel" on 22nd October, 1946.

After the shelling of Orion and Superb signals passed from the Admiralty to Admiral Willis, CinC Mediterranean. A signal on 21st October read "HMG wish to know whether the Albanians have learned to behave themselves" and asked whether any ships under command had passed through the North Strait since August. Willis's reply read "None have done so yet but my intention is that Admiral Kinahan, flying his flag in HMS Mauritius, with HMS Leander and two destroyers, should do so when they depart Corfu on 22nd October".

The cruisers, together with the destroyers Saumarez and Volage, sailed from Corfu on a course north, to proceed around the island and onwards to the Bay of Argostoli on the island of Cephalonia and rendezvous with the rest of the fleet for the annual Fleet Regatta. The ships were steaming in line ahead – Mauritius, then Saumarez, then Leander followed by Volage. Since the shelling in May all ships were at Action Stations with guns loaded ready to return any possible Albanian fire. They were in the centre of the swept channel, one mile wide and ten miles long, which led through the narrows between Corfu and Albania and out to the open sea. On the bridges binoculars scanned the coast for any sign of shell fire. Mauritius was only a mile from the coast at Denta Point and a turn to port was required to keep within the channel. Admiral Kinahan signalled a change to sail 310 degrees at 14.47. Two-and-a-half cables astern, Captain Selby, later Rear Admiral, on Saumarez gave the order to turn at 14.53 to keep in line astern.

HMS Saumarez mined amidships

Six minutes later a colossal explosion erupted beneath Saumarez, a few feet forward of the bridge, accompanied by huge brilliant yellow flashes. Saumarez lost steam and began to settle by the bows. She was drifting towards the coast out of the swept channel. She had struck a mine. She was on fire and sinking, with some crew killed and others wounded.

Kinahan signalled to Volage to try and take Saumarez in tow, and to Leander to return to Corfu and arrange whatever help would be needed.

Volage, some two miles astern, closed on Saumarez and managed to pass a line which was secured to her stern, but this later parted. While manoeuvring to pass another line the ships drifted very close and Volage suffered damage to her bow, caused by a stanchion slicing into her side. An inspection and repair team led by Sub-Lt HG Price RNVR was sent into Volage's bows to make her watertight. Volage was Price's first ship and he was just 19. At 1615 Price sent back one of his young stokers in response to assistance needed aft. This saved the stoker's life as seconds later there was another massive explosion. The tow line slackened and fell into the sea. Volage had also struck a mine. Forty feet of her bows had vanished, from the stem back to the front of "A" gun, square across the breadth of the ship. But the forward bulkhead had held and the ship was watertight and had power. The repair team were never seen again, together with two petty officers who had been on the forecastle deck.

HMS Volage mined in the bows

A third tow line was passed from the damaged forward of Volage to the stern of Saumarez and by going astern both ships cleared further mines. Saumarez's crew fought the fires as best they could without any power-pumped fire main. Eventually cables were passed across to provide lighting and power.

Once the ships were in the calmer waters of the narrow part of the North Channel the carrier HMS Ocean was able to provide much needed help – fire-fighting

Volage's bow damage

Saumarez being towed by Volage in line astern with cruiser Leander in lead

equipment and trained fire crews, foam-making machines and food and hot drinks. Boats carried the wounded, each with labelled injuries, across the choppy sea to Ocean where they went to the sick bay or the quarter deck which had been set up as an emergency treatment centre. They were still some five miles from Corfu where the wounded would be transferred to the hospital ship Maine which was underway from Malta.
The cruiser Leander then assisted in towing Volage and Saumarez into Corfu harbour.

It was now 0300 on 23 October. Forty-four British sailors had been killed and many injured, some with serious wounds, but there was little news coverage in the British press. Twelve crew members of Saumarez were buried in the Corfu British Cemetery but the others have no known grave.

Temporary repairs were undertaken in Corfu and the ships were towed to Malta for further work. Saumarez was later towed back to England and was scrapped. Volage had a new bow fitted in Malta and returned to sea duties on completion.

Very much more could be said about the mining, the loss of life, the brave acts and fine seamanship undertaken to get these damaged ships back to Malta, some 356 nautical miles distant. However, it is equally important to report on the incredibly protracted political and legal arguments that took place before proper resolution was achieved.

Firstly we needed to prove that the Albanians had laid the mines in an international seaway after it had been completely swept of the German mine field at the end of the war. A fleet of sweepers was sent to re-sweep the Channel and recover mines. On board was an independent observer, Cdr Mestre – the French delegate to the Medzon Board. Twenty-two mines were found. Three were exploded by rifle fire, two were recovered for examination, and the remainder were drifted to the Albanian shore. The mines were German Type GY containing 600 pounds of HE. It was known that the retreating Germans had left dumps of mines in Yugoslavia and they had been marked with a painted white swastika. These mines were so marked.

On 6th February 1948 an International Court at The Hague sat to hear the British and Albanians state their cases. The Albanians delayed and prevaricated and it was nine months before the British case was heard. Much play was made of the signal "Had the Albanians learned to behave themselves?" and things were not going well for us until a "mystery witness" was forthcoming. This was Lt Cdr Kovacic, late of the Yugoslav Navy. As a disillusioned officer he had seized a boat and sailed 200 miles across the Adriatic to Bari in southern Italy to tell the British authorities what he had seen. He had served on Yugoslav minesweepers and had seen these ships converted to mine laying and fully loaded with mines in Sibenik harbour on 17th October 1946. Sailing overnight they covered the 350 miles to lay their mines in the Corfu Channel before the British ships came through on 22nd October. The court found in favour of Britain and ordered that Albania was to pay £875,000 in compensation – that's £28 million pounds in today's money.
The Albanians would not settle for many years and the interminable delay was centred around the controversy of "The Gold".
Before the war Italy had lent gold to Albania but it had never been repaid. The retreating Germans took this gold with them and together with other lootings they held some 350 tons. A tripartite commission comprising Britain, France and the USA was set up with the task of returning this gold to the various rightful owners. Italy claimed her original pre-war loan and Albania claimed £600,000. Wrangling dragged on for years.

From time-to-time back-bench MPs raised the issue – e.g. in 1951 and 1981 -but it was not until 1996 that the gold was eventually returned to Albania and they settled the compensation ordered by the Court in The Hague. That's fifty years after the murder of 44 British seamen in the Corfu Channel on 22nd October 1946.

f any of you go to Corfu on holiday please take the time to visit the British Cemetery and pay your respects to some of my late shipmates. Thank you for your interest

(The author is a nonagenarian living in Chickerell who has been a member of our Society since 2008. Ed.)

The National Coastwatch Institution and Its Arrival at Portland Bill

by Roger Sutherland

For decades visual watch over the seas and coast around the British Isles was maintained by HM Coastguard. Much of this being manned from small lookouts positioned in areas deemed to be the most treacherous parts of the coast. With the rapid advances in technology such as radar, satellite navigation and VHF radio, the Maritime and Coastguard Agency (MCA) took the decision to close down these smaller stations. This resulted in there being no visual watch along some of the most treacherous stretches of the UK coast.

In 1994 tragedy struck when two fishermen on the Cadgwith Cove fishing boat lost their lives off the Cornish coast below a recently closed Coastguard lookout. This prompted local people to reopen and restore a visual watch. With the reopening of the first station at Bass Point on The Lizard the National Coastwatch Institution was born. The Station opened on 18 December 1994 and the official ceremony was carried out by the actress Jenny Agutter, who is now an Honorary Member.

NCI is a voluntary institution set up in 1994. Its aim is to restore a visual watch along UK shores following the closure of the many Coastguard lookouts. It is a registered charity managed by a Board of Trustees with a constitution agreed by the Charities Commission.

With its treacherous coastline and its position jutting out into the English Channel, The Isle of Portland is a major hazard to shipping. Over the centuries many ships have been wrecked along its shores and along the adjacent Chesil Beach.

The highest point overlooking Portland Bill is known as Branscombe Hill and this was considered the ideal location to site a Coastguard lookout, giving all-round vision of the west cliffs from Blacknor Point to Wallsend, the coastal path, the Bill Point and the notorious Portland Tidal Race, together with the dangerous waters that form off the Portland Ledges and the Shambles Bank. These factors were probably the reason for the Portland Bill Coastguard Station being one of the last to be closed in the early 90s.

The original station was built in 1934 as a full time (24 hour) station. During the 1970s the station was manned by auxiliaries and the watch hours reduced until eventually it was open only during daylight hours.

MCA underwent reorganisation resulting in the closure of the visual lookouts which were subsequently earmarked for demolition.

The Portland Station was saved from demolition by the intervention of local fisherman Ken Lynham, who, whilst walking his dog near the lookout, came upon contractors who were about to start work with their JCB. Being a member of the Southern Fishermen's Association, Ken had knowledge of the formation of the NCI and its work in the reopening of closed lookouts. Ken made contact with Capt Tony Starling Lark who had acquired some funding for rebuilds, and thus the station was saved.

Auxiliary Coastguard David Crabb agreed to take on the task of refurbishment of the lookout which, empty of all equipment, had been left to the mercy of the elements. He got volunteers to take on this daunting task but much finance was required and a massive fundraising appeal was launched.

Initial funding was given by the Weymouth Trawler Race, followed by a substantial grant from Eagle Star Insurance, through their subsidiary Navigators and **General.**

Refurbishing the Lookout 1996-97

NCI Portland Operational

In 1996 local volunteers led by David Crabb with additional assistance from a group from Raleigh International commenced the refurbishment, and on 23 May 1997 the lookout was re-opened and declared operational.

The refurbished watch room had not been enlarged and was able to accommodate only two watchkeepers at a time. Also, much more equipment was required, some of it bulky. Some was obtained from Coastguard storage and some was donated by members of the public. However, the refurbished building was too small and the bold decision was made to completely rebuild the station.

Rebuilding the Lookout

The Lookout Rebuilt

In 2001 a further fundraising campaign was launched and with a generous donation from The Valentines Trust the rebuild was commenced. Upon completion, the watch room had been increased to 12' 9" by 16' with a small kitchen, a toilet, stowage area, and a meeting room beneath.

Princess Anne's official visit

The rebuild was completed in 2004 and was dedicated by the Reverend Anita Thorne. On the 11 April 2006 the station was officially opened by HRH Princess Anne, The Princess Royal. During her visit she was able to watch the rescue of a yacht in distress in the Portland Race.

The increased size of the watch room accommodated a larger central chart table and desk area, allowing up to three watchkeepers to be on duty during a watch. During 2002 HM Coastguard awarded the Portland Bill Station 'Declared Facility Status'. This recognition making the station an integral part of the National Search and Rescue Organisation.

Initial training of new watch keepers was undertaken by our own training officers at the Coastguard Headquarters on Weymouth Quay. With the pending closure of the Portland Coastguard Headquarters and its incorporation into the new headquarters structure at Fareham, the decision was taken to build our own training centre within the station compound.

The Queen's Award for Voluntary Service

Building work was undertaken during May 2012, and on 2 June 2012 we celebrated its completion. At this time Station Manager Geoff Peters announced that we had been awarded the Queen's Award for Voluntary Service. (QAVS), and on 6 August 2012 we celebrated the Official Opening of the Training Centre together with the presentation of the Queen's Award. This award was not only for the Portland Station but included the other Dorset stations, these being St Albans Head, Lyme Bay and Peveril Point (Swanage).

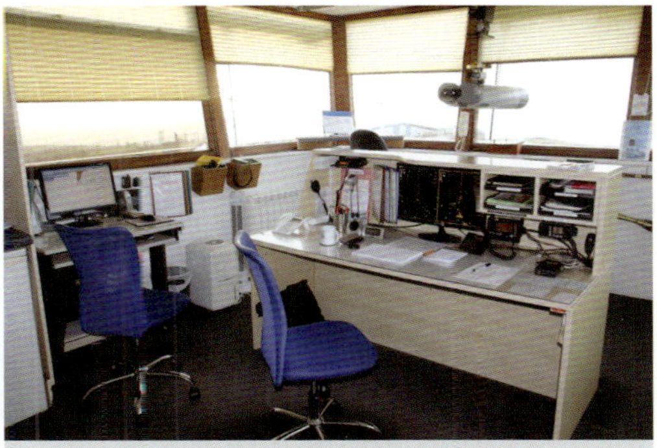

The new Watchroom

Once again we were honored to have HRH Princess Anne, accompanied by her husband Vice Admiral Sir Timothy Laurence, to perform the opening ceremony and present the awards. During their visit the Royal couple were given a tour of the watch room and the new training centre, and following the visit the Station Manager extended an invitation to both The Princess and her husband to become Honorary Watchkeepers. To everyone's delight the invitations were accepted.

Our location on Branscombe Hill gives us 360 degree all round vision of some 690 square miles of sea; including the west coast cliffs and coastal path, the notorious Portland Race which forms off the tip of The Bill, the Portland ledges and, to the east, the Shambles Bank. The station operates all year round with the exception of Christmas Day and Boxing Day, although we provide emergency cover for these days if HMCG requests.

A day is made up of three watches, split between 0700 hrs until 1900 hrs. Each watch being manned by three watchkeepers (two minimum). During winter months the opening hors are reduced to 0800 hrs to 1700 hrs.

Watchkeepers provide the eyes and ears along the coast, keeping a visual watch, monitoring radio channels, using radar and providing a listening watch in poor visibility.

A log of all water-based activities is kept during each watch and an hourly weather log is maintained throughout the day which is passed to HMCG at the beginning of each watch and at close down.

During each watch other activities such as walkers, horse riders and cliff climbers are closely observed.

To assist in our watchkeeping the Portland Bill station is equipped with a high power telescope, binoculars, three VHF Radios, one monitoring the Emergency Ch 16, one scanning all channels and the third monitoring Ch 65, the dedicated NCI channel. This channel is used for fishermen and sailors to receive updates on local weather and sea conditions in the area.

We also have radar, AIS (Automatic Identification System) and a weather station. All radio broadcasts are recorded, providing us with a back-up should May Day or Pan Pan messages be heard. A Web cam is located on the Portland Bill Lighthouse, controlled via a wireless link to the lookout which gives us a clear view on a monitor of the Inshore Passage used by sailors and fishermen to negotiate the rounding of the Bill, and the pathed areas around the Bill point used by walkers, enabling watch keepers to see the ledges, Pulpit Rock and the area around Red Crane regularly trodden by locals and

The Portland Race

visitors. Any incidents are recorded, thus providing HMCG with evidence should an inquiry be necessary. The Training Room is equipped with an overhead projector and drop-down screen, tables and chairs, white board and television. It can accommodate up to 40 persons to enable training sessions or lectures to be carried out. Solar Panels have been erected within the compound providing us with the necessary power to carry out the service we provide.

During station opening hours visitors are welcome to call in at the lookout to see what we do. This is provided the watch is not involved in an incident and will be at the discretion of the Watch Manager. Group visits with a presentation and tour of the watch-room can also be accommodated. These are normally done during an evening at watch close down. Alternatively, presentations can be arranged at group meeting places, after which invitations for group members to visit at a later date are often issued.

(Roger Sutherland is a Senior Watchkeeper at NCI Portland Bill and has been involved with the station since its inception. Ed.)

Poachers on the Border

By Jack Sweet

My grandmother Sweet was born Beatrice Sarah Martin at Oborne, in 1872, and although she lived for most of her 82 years over the county border in Yeovil, 55 of which were married to my very Somerset grandfather, she was always a 'Dorset girl'. The story I am about to relate happened on the county border and involved the forces of law and order on both sides.

There was a serious outbreak of poaching in the Sherborne and Yeovil areas during June and early July 1893 and the local police on both sides of the Dorset and Somerset border had been placed on poacher watch. One of the prime suspects was a Frederick Moors of South Barrow, and on Friday evening, 14 July he was seen in Sherborne in the company of James Lyne, a known convicted poacher. The local constabulary, sensing something was in the air, stepped up their patrols.

It was suspected that the poaching fraternity were regularly crossing the county boundary, and in the heightened state of alert four police officers were on patrol on both sides of Yeovil Bridge. Dorset officers, PC Miller from Nether Compton and PC Meech of Yetminster had concealed themselves behind hedges at the bottom of Babylon Hill, whilst PCs Marsh and Wise from Yeovil had taken up station on the Somerset side of the bridge.

Shortly before half-past five on the following Saturday morning a horse and trap was observed coming at a steady trot down Babylon Hill, and as it approached the bridge the Dorset officers recognised Moors as the driver and the convicted poacher Lyne as his passenger. The constables stepped into the road but as PC Miller held up his hands for the driver to stop Moors swerved the trap around the officer and urged the horse into a gallop. PC Meech, who was standing behind his colleague, tried to seize the reins from the driver but missed and fell under the trap. Meech was knocked unconscious and dragged for several yards before one of the wheels ran over him.

The trap sped over Yeovil Bridge and PCs Marsh and Wise had to jump for their lives as it was driven furiously at them and away up the Sherborne Road to Yeovil. However, the two constables managed to glimpse a large bag in the back of the trap.

All this was witnessed by dairyman Thomas Score who lived by Yeovil Bridge, and who would later corroborate the police officers' statements in court and would confirm that there was a large bag in the back of the trap.

PC Meech recovered consciousness but was badly hurt and bleeding heavily from a head wound. He was taken to a nearby house and Dr Williams was called from Sherborne. The doctor found the officer suffering from a deep scalp wound, severe laceration to his back where the wheel had passed over him and heavy bruising to his legs and shoulders.

Later that day Frederick Moors and James Lyne were arrested at their homes and on 20 July, they were brought before the Sherborne Magistrates charged with causing grievous bodily harm to PC Meech. The events of the Saturday morning were recalled by the prosecution who stated that the police officers had tried to detain the prisoners on suspicion of poaching. The four constables described their actions and those of the prisoners. The Bench was told that as PC Miller called for the driver to stop the trap, the prisoner Lyne had shouted " Drive over the -------s if they won't get out of the way!". The dairyman, Thomas Score, took the stand and recalled what he had witnessed as he stood on Yeovil Bridge. Yeovil solicitor, Mr W Marsh, defending, stated that before the police had the right to stop his clients they must have good cause to suspect that they had come from land where they had been in search of game. The fact that James Lyne had been convicted of poaching did not justify the attempts to stop his clients without proper authority, and the police must take the consequences of their actions. His clients had been lawfully driving to Yeovil with a bag of mushrooms and when the constables had jumped into the road, the horse had taken fright, the reins had broken, and the horse had bolted out of control, accidently knocking down PC Meech. Mr Marsh therefore sought the dismissal of the charges. However, the magistrates committed the prisoners for trial but allowed bail at £25 each with two sureties of £25.

Frederick Moors and James Lyne appeared at the Dorset October Quarter Sessions charged with causing grievous bodily harm to PC Meech. Once again the defence was put forward that as there was no proof that the pair had been on a poaching expedition, the police had no authority to arrest them, and the injuries to the constable were not the result of an unlawful act. However, the jury found them guilty as charged and Moors and Lyne were each sentenced to nine months hard labour. In pronouncing the sentence, Mr Hastings Middleton, the Chairman of Quarter Sessions, stated that this had been a most serious assault and the result of driving at a man in this way could have led to the prisoners standing in the dock charged with manslaughter or even murder.

PC Meech was incapacitated for six weeks, but made a full recovery.

Thomas Phipps Howard - a Soldier with Wellington

by Carl Whitehouse

Church memorials can often lead one to discover unexpected and fascinating aspects of history. One such example is the memorial in St. Mary's Church Weymouth to a Major-General Thomas Phipps Howard, KH, KCH, who died in October 1847 in his eightieth year.

The brief details on the monument give little hint of the eventful life of a man who fought in the revolutionary and Napoleonic wars. His obituary in "The Gentleman's Magazine" mentions that he joined the Royal York Hussars in 1793, soon after the execution of Louis XVI in France. This was a time when Britain was deeply concerned about the proclamation of a French Republic, and the spread of revolutionary ideas. The French had declared war on Britain on 1 February 1793 and young men, like the twenty-five year old Phipps Howard, sought to join up to repel them. He was gazetted as a Cornet that year, at which time he was living in Grosvenor Square, London.

Many people were seeking to raise corps of troops, but in a very disorganised fashion in different places, thereby causing confusion. It seems that Phipps Howard had contacts with a Colonel de Sinclair who was seeking to raise troops in Brussels ready to transport anywhere the government might wish, but the government were not yet ready for this. A letter to the Home Office sent on November 20th 1793, shows the young man's frustration and enterprise.

He wrote: "Sir, Not being permitted to be useful to Government in a military line, by Colonel de Sinclair having met with a refusal in his offer to raise a legion, I am determined as much as lies in my power, to serve the cause of Royalty, in another manner until I can be fortunate as once more to see the camp. Knowing that government wished to have His Majesties most gracious proclamation distributed in France, I have caused to be printed at Bruxelles several copies and have been so fortunate as to get them conveyed to, and circulated about Paris, by the same means I can get anything conveyed to, or from, that unhappy city. I have also sent them to Gwent, Liege and Aix-la-Chapelle. Should this information be of any use to forward any plans government may have in agitation, you have but to command. Sir, your most obedient and most humble servant. *Thos. Phipps Howard, 43 Park Street Grosvenor Square."*

He also sent the Home office an unsigned letter he had received from a Walloon merchant at Verviers, reporting on his distribution in France of British and Dutch proclamations, announcing the execution of the Duc d'Orléans, and offering to pass on further intelligence. This sounds as if he was becoming part of an early spy network. Phipps Howard did serve briefly on the continent, but by 1795 he had been promoted Lieutenant in the Royal York Hussars. This regiment was about to be sent to the West Indies, where a slave rebellion had broken out in Haiti (then called the French colony of St. Domingue). He travelled with his regiment and during his time in Haiti wrote a journal. This has since been edited and published as "The Haitian Journal of Lieutenant Howard, York Hussars, 1796-1798". The journal gives a detailed account of the rebellion which had started in 1791 when slaves, inspired by the revolutionary concepts in France about the rights of man, had risen up against the white planters. The planters, who supported the French royalists, sought help from the British, as well as from the Spanish who occupied the other half of the island of Hispaniola. The rebels were led by a brilliant strategist, Toussaint Louverture, but initially they were hard-pressed on all sides. Following the declaration of a republic in France the situation changed markedly because the French revolutionary powers were in favour of the abolition of slavery. As a result Louverture had an ally in the French expeditionary force. Over the next few years, whilst Thomas Phipps Howard was serving in the country, they slowly overcame the Spanish and British forces, even though poorly armed and often starving. It was said the former slaves showed extraordinary courage and combativeness to prevent a restoration of slavery, even battling with stones and bare hands when they lacked ammunition.

The British were eventually defeated in April 1798, and as a result Phipps Howard returned to Britain. Sadly, after the defeat, the French sought to re-establish control over the colony, not allowing any say to Toussaint Louverture and those who had battled so courageously with him. In 1801, Louverture responded by issuing a constitution for St. Domingue that called for black autonomy and a sovereign black state. He decreed that he would be governor-for-life. Napoleon Bonaparte, then in charge in France, immediately sent a large force to restore French rule. After a successful campaign they promised Louverture his freedom if he agreed to integrate his remaining troops in the French army. In 1802 he accepted these terms. However, he was deceived, seized and transported to France where he died in 1804. By then other black Haitians had seized power, massacred the remaining white settlers and proclaimed a republic in the year of Louverture's death.

Thomas Phipps Howard saw none of this. After his return to Britain he was promoted Captain and in 1803 he transferred to the 23rd Light Dragoons. The next year he married Margaret Rae the daughter of Sir David Rae, Bart. an eminent Scots advocate who had been made Lord Chief Justice Clerk in 1799, and created a baronet in

1804. This was presumably a good match, and they would be married for 43 years.

Five years later war had broken out again and in June 1809 Phipps Howard embarked for Lisbon to join Wellington's forces in the Peninsular War. By July 27th that year the British army was 75 miles from Madrid and engaged in the Battle of Talavera. During this the 23rd Light Dragoons proved somewhat undisciplined. They broke into a wild gallop running into a hidden ravine, hobbling many horses and then, having charged past infantry positions who easily fended them off, they ran into the French cavalry. Forty-nine were killed, fifty wounded, and many others taken prisoner. The regiment had to be sent home to refit. Thomas Phipps Howard was among the wounded left on the field and taken prisoner. He would remain a French prisoner until the end of the war in 1814, although he would be promoted major in 1810.

He is next heard of arriving at the prisoner-of-war camp at Verdun in May 1811. Verdun was probably the largest French prisoner-of-war camp for captured British officers. These prisoners had considerable freedom there, but were obliged to sign a paper, promising upon honour to conform to the regulations of the depot, and not to escape if they were permitted to reside in the town. He would remain in Verdun until 1814, and the first defeat and exile of Napoleon.

He then returned to his regiment, but The 23rd Light Dragoons were disbanded at Radipole barracks in Weymouth in 1817. This probably explains how Thomas Phipps Howard came to live in the town. He retired from active service the following year on a half-pay pension of £200 p.a., and was promoted to Lieutenant-Colonel. Sometime around this period he was made a Knight of the Royal Guelphic Order. This was an order under the Crown of Hanover that the Prince Regent (later George IV) had inaugurated in 1815. Although a knight, it did not give the honorific title of "Sir". Some years later he would be promoted to Knight Commander in the same order, and thus was able to have the initials KH, KCH after his name.

Phipps Howard now settled in in Weymouth and by 1838 was a county magistrate, having been further promoted to Colonel. In that year we find him once again writing to the Home Office, but with a very different request. This time it was to report a case of arson, destroying agricultural produce belonging to George Luckham of Radipole, as well as unsuccessful arson attacks in Wyke Regis and Fleet. He asks the government to provide a reward for the apprehension of the culprit. The government agreed and a reward of £100 was offered, very large for the time. Phipps Howard, ever ready to use his pen, wrote back thanking the Secretary of State and enclosing a copy of the poster offering the reward which had been circulated throughout the neighbourhood. He went on to say how this offer had shown that the government was very concerned for the protection of property. One must remember that at this time Arson as a crime was still subject to the death penalty, although probably more often the result would have been transportation.

The Tolpuddle Martyrs trial had taken place just four years previously, and this was a further reminder that all was not well in industrial relations on Dorset farms, but it is not known if the culprit was apprehended.

Thomas Howard Phipps was promoted major-general in a further general promotion of the army in 1846, but he died a year later at his home in Royal Terrace near the Kings Statue, after an adventurous, if troubled, life. His remains were buried in the 'catacombs' of Holy Trinity Church but his monument was put up in the parish church of St. Mary's. Seven years later his wife, Margaret, died and is also remembered in the memorial.

Weymouth & Melcombe Regis in the Early Nineteenth Century

by Carl Whitehouse

The visits of George III made Weymouth a fashionable resort, but he visited the town for the last time in 1805. He never saw the statue erected to honour his Golden Jubilee in 1810. His granddaughter, Princess Charlotte, did come to the town in 1814, and visited three times over the next two years. She took great interest in the town, going out to visit Royal Navy ships in the bay and arranging for her chaplain, the Bishop of Salisbury, to lay the foundation stone of the new parish church (St. Mary's, in St. Mary Street) in October 1815. Sadly, Charlotte died in childbirth in 1817 and Royal interest in the town ended. Her father, George IV, succeeded to the throne in 1820. He preferred Brighton to Weymouth, and the Royal property, Gloucester House and its furnishings were sold off. The town now needed to advertise itself to encourage continued interest and, over the next few years, several new guides were published to tell of its beauties and facilities.

The town was extending, the population increasing from 4117 to 6622 between 1811 and 1821 and reaching 7700 by the 1841 Census. At this time over 230 were seamen, However, a large part of the population were providing services: 44 bakers, 105 tailors, 134 bootmakers and 89 carpenters. 766 were Domestic servants of which 84% were women, and domestic service accounted for 60% of all women in work.

Many of the bricklayers, carpenters and similar trades would have been involved in building, although by this time much of the seafront was complete. Belvedere and Brunswick Terrace had been built in the 1820's followed in the next decade by Frederick Place and Waterloo Place.

Many of these properties were boarding houses for visitors to the town. The 1830's Guide which describes Weymouth and its neighbourhood and "every place in the county of Dorset worthy of the observation of strangers" mentions these ranges "as most desirable, from their vicinity to the place of bathing, public-rooms, libraries, and theatre" and says that from the windows fronting the sea, is a most delightful prospect: the mountainous hills and chalky cliffs on the left, which stretch upwards of twenty miles from west to east, exhibit a magnificent sketch of nature". The guide then describes the facilities: "Horses with pillions may be procured; and a number of cars drawn by donkeys, and donkeys with side-saddles, are always in attendance near the bathing-place, for ladies who prefer this mode of enjoying the sea air, or who are obliged to have recourse to it through indisposition."

The esplanade was considered "unquestionably one of the grandest marine walks in Europe: it is nearly three quarters of a mile in length, and thirty feet wide; it assimilates to a quarter circle in shape, and is banked up and railed off from the sands by 336 stone posts and 4,620 feet of iron chain". A few of those stone posts still exist by the Pier Bandstand, but sadly no railings now.

The guidebook continues, in grand style, "In a calm summer evening, during spring tides, it is impossible to describe the beauties of this enchanting parade: the vast concourse of genteely-dressed company, enjoying the cool refreshing breeze, the rippling of the water, the distant view of the yachts and ships in the roads, the bold white cliffs and lofty hills surrounding the bay, and, not unfrequently, shoals of mackerel, or other small fish, close up to the wall of the Esplanade conspire to make this a most interesting and delightful promenade.

It wasn't always so idyllic Weymouth and Portland can see more extreme weather. On the morning of the 23rd of November, 1824, a major gale "coming from different points of the compass, caused a sudden perpendicular flow of the sea, to the height of five feet above the ordinary spring tides and the greater part of the Esplanade was demolished". According to another observer "Whole rows of houses that fronted the foaming, raging, billows, were completely inundated; the pride of Melcombe, its beautiful esplanade, was nearly all demolished, the stone posts and chains were rent up and entirely broken".

Fortunately, this was a rarity. The town could still attract people to the beach and the bathing, although modern bathers may not recognise the advice given. "The most proper time for bathing is early in the morning, fasting, and before any exercise be taken; perfect repose of body and serenity of mind, being equally suited to give effect to the end proposed. To bathe late in the day, (more especially in hot weather) will occasion great depression of the spirits, particularly in debilitated or paralytic persons. As a guide to bathers, it may generally be observed, that if after coming out of the sea, the spirits are exhilarated, and an universal glow is felt throughout the system, the immersion has had its beneficial effect. if contrary sensations be felt, bathing should not be persisted in.

Bathing was from bathing machines drawn into the water by horses. There were about forty machines in the 1830's and horses were available from six o'clock in the morning in summer.

If visitors didn't want to face the sea, there was an indoor bathing establishment, or they could travel two and a half miles out to a spa at Nottington, said to be "deservedly famous for its mineral spring". The water at the spa house there was said to have "a strong foetid sulphureous smell, not much unlike gunpowder newly enflamed, and a flavour resembling boiled eggs". A local doctor, Dr. Pickford, wrote, "That in disorders of the stomach, liver, and spleen, these waters are of the most eminent service, by searching the most minute ramifications of the capillaries, which are too frequently the seat of the disease. They give energy to the whole muscular fibre, and an exhilaration to the spirits, which are never witnessed from the administration of ordinary means under similar circumstances."

The growth of the town necessitated new infrastructure. The bridge over the harbour between Weymouth and Melcombe needed improving. An 1820's guide reported that the original handsome structure of wood had become very much dilapidated and dangerous. Following anAn Act of Parliament, the foundation-stone of a new stone bridge, with a swing in the centre, for the passage of ships to the upper part of the harbour was laid on the 10th of September 1821,. This would eventually be replaced by the present Town Bridge over a century later.

In 1828 the commissioners for lighting and watching the town approved plans to change lighting from oil to gas to gas lamps, only 20 years after the first demonstration of gas street-lighting in Pall Mall, London. The gas works to provide for this would be built on the Marsh in Weymouth with the gas conveyed to the town through a tunnel of 500 feet in length, under the Backwater.

By the 1830's it was decided the town needed a new Guildhall. Ellis, in his 1829 "History of the Antiquities of Weymouth" described the old guildhall in St. Edmund Street as a "plain inelegant structure with evident tokens of a deficiency of taste in its architectural erection". The new Guildhall would be built in classical style in 1836-7.

Two years earlier the Corporation began another grand project. They decided to build a large new park at the entrance to the town. 50 acres were acquired between the road to Dorchester and the backwater and an embankment wall was started at a cost of £1000.

The first stone was laid on the 4th of June, 1834, the day being celebrated as a general holiday with shops closed and all business suspended. A grand dinner was served in the National school room followed in the evening by a ball. The poor were not forgotten and "enjoyed abundance of good old English fare, roast beef and plum pudding," whilst the curate of St. Mary's treated the children of the National school with 500 buns. For various reasons the Park never materialised and in the end the land was sold off for housing and commercial businesses which became the Park District in the town today.

Another idea was to enclose a large harbour between Weymouth and Portland with a breakwater. This would take many years before the idea was accepted but in 1849 Prince Albert laid the foundation stone.

It wasn't only the Corporation responding to the increased population and opportunities. George Chamberlayne, the Rector of Wyke Regis, was concerned that people in his parish on the Weymouth side of the harbour had too far to travel to church. At his own expense he decided to build a new church by the harbourside. As he had already donated £500 for the rebuilding of St. Mary's in 1817, he must have been a rich man. The first stone of the church, to be called Holy Trinity, was laid on 1st September 1834. It was big enough to hold 1000 people and a 'National School', supported by the Church, would be built next door. St. Mary's, the Parish church for Melcombe Regis, held up to 2000 people. As well as the Parish churches, Weymouth Baptist Church was built in 1813, and there was an Independent chapel in St. Nicholas Street on the Melcombe side, from which a 'Little Meeting' on the Weymouth side emerged and built their own chapel in 1822, now known as Hope Chapel. There were Methodist meetings in Conygar Place, (now called Lower Bond Street), and elsewhere in the town. The religious life of the town was well catered for.

In 1829 Parliament passed the Catholic Emancipation Act, this was supported by three local MP's, including Thomas Fowell Buxton, but was not popular in the town. The fourth MP, Colonel John Gordon, voted against the Bill, and 1233 local people sent Him a vote of thanks to his fellow MP, congratulating him on his stance, and finishing with a rather intolerant statement:

"But Sir, while we repeat to you our warmest thanks, we cannot forbear saying that we do feel a pride and gratification, in finding one at least of our four representatives in the list of that glorious minority, the real organ of the national voice, who keeping themselves pure from the pestilential contagion of modern liberality, have resolutely stood up in the cause of everlasting truth, and strenuously resisted, to the last, the enactment of that law which opens a broad way for the re-entrance and establishment of a tyrannical and idolatrous religion in this STILL FREE AND PROTESTANT KINGDOM."

Despite this prejudice there was already a Catholic congregation in Weymouth. In 1820, a French emigré priest, Abbé Simon had taken up residence at 63 St Mary Street, just opposite St. Mary's, and began saying Mass there. His congregation rapidly reached 50, which led to objections from his landlord because of the crowding, but the group continued to grow. In 1829 Father Hartley arrived and bought a site on the Dorchester Road where a church and presbytery could be built, and St. Augustine's church was opened there in October 1835.

The National Schools have already been mentioned. These were founded by the National Society for Promoting Religious Education, set up in 1811 to provide elementary education to the children of the poor, in accordance with the teaching of the Church of England. There were also schools founded by the British and Foreign School Society, the successor of the Lancasterian Society founded in 1808 to educate children according to the principles of the educational reformer , Joseph Lancaster, whose famous meeting with George III is celebrated in a plaque in Weymouth library, originally set in the wall of St. Mary's School.

In Melcombe, a Lancasterian school had been opened in 1813, at an expense of more than £1000. However, due to a failure of subscriptions, the committee was unable to liquidate the debt. The committee of St. Mary's National School, just being formed, took the debt upon themselves and took the school over. In 1819 a grant from the National Society enabled them to pay the arrears and build a girl's school adjoining the boy's school. By 1845 St. Mary's schools, situated in Maiden Street, close to the church, provided for 270 boys and 270 girls.

Monuments in churches such as St. Mary's remind one of the fragility of early 19th Century life. One monument is to a Mary Ellis who died at the age of 16 in 1832, "a tribute of unavailing grief to the cherished memory of a much loved child", whilst another, to Thomas Henry Martin, a graduate of Christ's College Cambridge, who died at the age of 29 in 1835, shows the depth of loss felt by the parents who, it records, "lived in, and doated on him".

A heart-wrenching monument is that to the three children of Richard & Emily Wardell who died of scarlet fever within three weeks of October 1843, aged 3, 5 and 6. Such losses of young people highlight the state of public health at the time. During the 1830's and 1840's England suffered many major epidemics ranging from influenza to typhoid and cholera, whilst children were subject to epidemics of measles, diphtheria, whooping cough and scarlet fever. One report suggests that a half of all children of farmers, labourers, artisans and servants died before the age of 5. In the parish of Radipole and Melcombe Regis church registers for 1843 show 120 baptisms and 17 infant deaths, suggesting an infant mortality of 142/1000. Mortality for children under 5 was 267/1000. On this evidence Weymouth was one of the better areas in the country, but still liable to epidemics.

People often had only limited health care facilities. In Weymouth a public dispensary was set up for the relief of the sick poor in October 1816. Supported by voluntary contributions, it was initially conducted at the premises of a widow Groves, at 10 St. Mary Street, but later moved to Maiden Street. Within a few years nearly four thousand people had been relieved, and about four hundred children a year were vaccinated against smallpox, the only immunisation available at that time.

To raise funds for the Dispensary, sermons were preached in the parish church. Eminent people came to deliver them. In 1818 it was the Bishop of Gloucester, and ten years later the Bishop of Bristol. The report on the latter's sermon adds that the next day he was guest of honour at an elegant evening party. He was clearly mixing business with pleasure, but one hopes those at the party contributed well!
There were no hospitals in Weymouth at this stage, although the Dispensary was also called an infirmary. Dorset County Hospital in Dorchester was founded as a charity for the working poor in 1840. Only in 1848 was a Sanatorium provided in Weymouth. Based in Clarence Buildings and supported by rich benefactors, its whole ethos would be taking care of those who couldn't pay.

If people couldn't care for themselves, and couldn't pay for care, the option was to apply to the parish for poor law relief, which might include admission to a workhouse. The system was working poorly and in 1834 a Poor Law Amendment Act was passed to curb the cost and address abuses of the old system. Under this Act, Poor Law Unions were to be set up, and relief would only be given in workhouses, where conditions would be such as to deter any but the truly destitute from applying for relief. The Weymouth Poor Law Union was formed in January 1836, and soon after erected the Weymouth Union workhouse on Wyke Road. The building still stands, having become Portwey Hospital and then converted into residences. The conditions in these workhouses were intended to be harsh, but the system survived for 100 years.

Weymouth and Melcombe Regis were no doubt typical of many similar towns. The Esplanade and seafront provided a beautiful resort for the rich, exemplified in the 1842 print showing the hot-air balloon 'Albion', piloted by Mr. Green and Capt. Currie taking off on a flight towards Bere Regis. The Corporation and churches were trying to provide modern facilities and educational facilities for the people of the town as well as for visitors, but behind this there was still much poverty and consequent public health problems.

In the 1840's the Royal Navy would establish a base at Portland and a decade later a railway would at last reach Weymouth. These would change the character of the town and make it a resort for others than the fashionable rich, but its Georgian elegance would remain.

Portland Bird Observatory and Field Centre

Nicholas Wright

The Old Lower Light at Portland Bill has been the home of the Portland Bird Observatory and Field Centre since 1961. Because of its geographical position, being approximately mid-way along Britain's south coast and protruding some six miles out into the English Channel, The Isle of Portland has always been a major route for migrating birds, moths and butterflies - their first landfall as they come north from France in spring, and their last filling station as they head south across La Manche in the autumn.

Animal migration has of course been studied since the nineteenth century but it was only fairly recently, especially during the nineteen thirties, forties and fifties, that serious and extensive zoological work really got under way. Since then the study of animal behaviour, distribution and movement patterns has expanded significantly and a wealth of scientific data has been accrued.

Pioneering migration study at Portland started in 1951 when Dr. Ken Rooke and friends began working at the Bill. For a decade these stalwarts endured temporary accommodation in caravans, in the old RN Wireless Station, and even in underground caves in Southwell before they were able to secure the proper and permanent premises of the Old Lower Light.

The Old Lower Light - *Watercolour by Patricia Adams*

The nineteen fifties saw the establishment of many bird observatories in Britain, chiefly along the coasts, and today there are eighteen in total. Portland is one of the most important and is probably the busiest. It is a registered scientific charity governed by trustees and it has two full-time members of staff – the Warden and his assistant.

As a field centre it offers basic hostel-style self-catering accommodation for up to 24 people and in an average year it will take around 2500 resident visitors, drawn from a mix of professional zoologists, amateur naturalists, and school and university study groups. It also boasts a paid-up membership of some 800 people, again a mix of professional zoologists and amateur naturalists, who come from all over the UK, Europe, and from even further afield.

The Observatory owns the freehold of the Old Lighthouse and associated buildings plus some 40 acres of adjacent land. On this land it grows trees and wild shrubs as cover for the passing bird populations, and it farms crops, especially seed crops, for birds and small mammals under the principles of "farming for wildlife". The Observatory is open every day, all year round but it is not a designated nature reserve, although visitors are welcome, but preferably by prior arrangement.

One sees Portland as a large and rather barren mass of old hard limestone with relatively little vegetation and one assumes that it might be the home of various seabirds but probably but not much else. Wrong!

Yes. There are of course nesting seabirds: herring gulls, kittiwakes, razorbills, guillemots and a few puffins, and there are some nesting fulmars, peregrines and ravens on the cliffs. And in winter there are many sea ducks, scoters, divers, skuas, shearwaters and all sorts of gulls plus quite a few visiting raptors and waders. There are also the usual song and garden birds in the domestic gardens of the small towns and villages and in the hedgerows and copses on the limited farmland.

However, Portland is famous for the vast numbers of migrating passerines (perching and songbirds) passing through each spring and autumn and visiting from the Continent in winter.

Spring migration usually starts in early March with chiffchaffs and willow warblers heading north, and a bit later these are supplemented by reed, sedge and garden warblers, and whitethroats, plus goldcrests, wagtails, finches, whinchats, stonechats, wheatears, redstarts, robins and other thrushes., and sometimes rarities such as wrynecks. And of course the swallows, martins and swifts come through in large numbers overhead.

A Goldcrest pops up to say, "Good Morning" and Wrynecks always look startled.

Movement is chiefly at night and depending upon weather conditions a "drop" of hundreds of warblers can often be found early morning in the Observatory grounds. Spring migration peters-out by mid-May.

And then it all starts again in July with the onset of the autumn migration! This lasts until well into October and often brings more variety than the spring.

The winter routine includes a regular check on the visiting waders and sea birds in Portland Harbour and at Ferrybridge (the southern end of The Fleet) – Brent Geese, Mergansers, Eiders and other sea ducks, Scoters, Great Northern and Red-Throated Divers, grebes and petrels etc.

A rare Leach's Petrel competes in Portland Harbour.

The Observatory grounds are well-wooded with specially grown short trees and shrubs. Paths have been cut through these across which are placed mist nets, into which the birds fly when roused by the warden or his assistants on their regular rounds. The nets do not harm or damage the captive birds which are taken in small linen bags to the ringing room where they are weighed, measured, recorded, and ringed by well qualified and specially licenced ringers, and then released. The nets are never left unattended.

To date over 200,000 birds of more than 200 species have been ringed and over the years a vast database of movement patterns, dates, and distances has been built up through reported recoveries – that's ringed birds either re-trapped elsewhere or later found dead around UK, Europe or Africa and the ring details reported to London's Natural History Museum. Valuable data has also been built up concerning the longevity of different species. These data bases are all computerised. Nowadays the Observatory rings between 8000 and 9000 birds in an average year.

The Observatory has a number of distinguished entomologists among its membership and a detailed study of moth and butterfly migration is maintained. The moths and butterflies use the same routes as the birds! Numbers and movements of the larger species – Painted Lady, Red Admiral, Peacock, Comma, Small Tortoiseshell, Brimstone and Clouded Yellow etc – are noted along with details of the blues, the browns, the skippers and the whites. Visiting vagrants such as the Monarch, the Camberwell Beauty and the Large Tortoiseshell have also been recorded.

A Camberwell Beauty

A Death's Head Hawk Moth Larva and Imago.

Moth traps are put out each night and good numbers of large and micro moths are examined, recorded and released each morning.

So, the Old Lower Light is a very busy place and I hope that this article has aroused your interest. Why not call-up its website which is updated daily "portlandbirdobs.com". Or if you'd like to drop-in do please phone Martin Cade, the Warden, on 01305 820533.

The author served as a Trustee of the Observatory from 2005 to 2013 and as Secretary to the Trustees from 2007 to 2013.

All photos by Martin Cade.

Modern Medieval Tiles from Stoborough

by John Neimer

You could be forgiven for thinking that the photo above was a section of the floor of one of Dorset's ancient churches or some other medieval establishment. This conclusion is understandable as is the assumption that these are ancient artefacts created centuries ago but somehow well preserved.

You would be wrong on both counts! These beautiful objects were made in Dorset by an artist who is very much alive and it depicts, in fact, her fireplace! She and her husband create these lovely things in their small workshop in a Dorset village using the skills developed in restoration projects around the country.
As you might imagine, the process of manufacture of these replica medieval inlaid tiles is a long and very painstaking one. In order to replicate tiles of a particular period and of a particular locality, the correct clay has to be sourced, the moulds and patterns made, the slip clay and glazes mixed and, for some organisations, historically correct techniques must be used.

The clay, for example, must be of a uniform and fine texture, malleable and easily worked. It is first worked to the right consistency then left to 'sour' for twenty four hours. Then it is moulded into the rough size and shape to fit the mould and here the true skill of the medieval tile and pattern makers is revealed; an accurate allowance must be made for the clay to shrink during the process of manufacture; this can be up to ten percent but varies with the type of clay being used. This skill is to be noted also in the form of the tiles where the edges are chamfered to allow the lime mortar on which they were laid to rise up between them to lock them in place as it sets.

The clay is pressed into the mould so as to fill every corner and void. Then the pattern is pressed into the clay leaving an indented impression in the surface. The impression in the tile is filled with 'slip', a semi-liquid clay mixture, which forms the design of the tile. In order to ensure that all the trapped air is expelled from the slip the tile is tapped and any indentations left by the bubbles bursting smoothed over. To ensure no bubbles are left the tile is left to stand for twenty four hours, this is vital as any trapped bubbles would burst during firing and ruin the tile. At this time also four indentations or 'keys' will be cut into the back of the tile to assist in anchoring it to the base layer of mortar on which it will be laid.

After drying to the 'leather dry' state the excess slip is scraped from the surface and the tiles are left to dry for three or four weeks. When they are completely dry glaze is brushed onto the surface and they are fired.

The reader will appreciate that manufacturing tiles using these traditional methods is a lengthy process requiring much intricate work. In the above account I have made frequent mention of the 'pattern' better known by tile makers as the 'stamp'. The stamp is the basis of the whole process and this part of the operation demands great skill and patience on the part of the pattern maker. Once again, the initial part of the process is the selection of the right material; i.e., the choice of timber. It requires a close grain and must be readily worked. Oak, for example, tends to split, beech is often used whilst holly lends itself to highly detailed stamps but will split when it absorbs water from the clay. Furthermore the method of working is important; using the long grain is easier but will not lend itself to fine detail so that the favourite area is the end grain. The illustration below are the patterns for a set of four tiles that make up a single complex design, they are made from the end grain of a piece of holly and the splits from moisture absorbance can be seen. The detail that can be achieved by the pattern maker is extraordinary.

Diana's interest in medieval tiles was prompted by request from a local museum, she studied the techniques needed to produce replica medieval tiles and thus acquired the skills and interest to pursue this aspect of the tiler's art.

The illustration above depicts tiles decorated using a different method. Here the smoothed, fired tile is printed using a pattern block, made of polystyrene, with a coloured oxide glaze on it, leaving the design imprinted on the surface. The tile is then fired. As you see, tiles produced by this method can be very intricate and beautiful but must not be confused with the medieval inlaid tile.

The lovely things described here are made in Stoborough by Diana Hall and her husband John, she is the tiler and he makes the stamps. Her interest in tiling was initially sparked by a friend, Peggy Angus (1904 – 1993), the artist and designer of hand printed wall paper and tiles (see Wikipedia) who suggested that she design the tiles for her new kitchen floor and, following the success of that, to designing a number of bespoke tiled floors in partnership with Peggy. The tiles designed and used for those projects were of the printed variety (see above) not the medieval inlaid kind described elsewhere in this article.

There are other people in the country who make replica medieval tiles but Diana is the only one who uses the authentic medieval processes from finding the correct clay to the production methods described in this article. Diana's and John's work can be seen in Winchester and Ely cathedrals and several other ecclesiastical establishments.

Sadly, the Victorians, in their enthusiasm for restoring churches to their neo-Gothic ideas tore up whole sections of worn flooring and replaced them with tiles of the correct design made by Minton and other 19th century manufacturers. They employed the tools and machinery they used to make their commercial products and the results can be seen in many English churches. They give some idea of what a medieval floor would have looked like but at the same time have a mechanical uniformity and perfection that betrays their origin. In contrast, when you see an area of floor restored using Diana's tiles, they do, of course, look newer than the surrounding floor but that would be the only difference.

Fortunately antiquarians carefully collected the discarded tiles and the British Museum holds an extensive collection of them and has a comprehensive catalogue (see the bibliography below).

So next time you are in one of those ancient buildings don't just admire the stonework or the brass tomb plates, have a look at the floor, it might surprise you!

Bibliography

Medieval Tiles: Hans Van Lemmen published by Shire Publications of Princes Risborough.

Elizabeth Eames: Catalogue of Medieval Tiles published by British Museum Publications Ltd

Memories of a Vicar's Wife in Rural North Dorset

By Dorothy McNeish

Over the years I have lived in many homes of different sizes and designs but my favourite was The Rectory in a sleepy village in North Dorset where we moved to in the mid-70s. Built in 1934 (the year my husband was born) it stood in about one third of an acre with two large lawns, one of which was a former tennis court. We had two large vegetable plots, and one year I was proud to keep the family in vegetables for a whole six months. There were also apple and plum trees as well as soft fruit bushes. From the generous bay window in the sitting room we had a wonderful view across the gentle valley to the neighbouring village, a view which, sadly, changed drastically with the onset of Dutch Elm Disease. The house had everything a young family needed, with a spacious interior and plenty of room for visitors and guests.

You may wonder how a Moonraker (from Wiltshire), and an Episcopalian from Glasgow, came to spend five happy years in a Dorset village. We were settling into parish life after my husband had left the Royal Air Force as a chaplain and was offered the benefice of three rural village parishes. Never before had he experienced village life yet he quickly came to love it. He bought himself a bike and thoroughly enjoyed the opportunity of being able to stop at any time to chat to his parishioners as he rode around. Indeed, the cycling habit later became a favourite hobby after retirement.

A great benefit of being village clergy is that one gets to know everyone whether church members or not. I was amazed at a social function when a local farmer asked my husband if he knew all the people present. He looked around and answered "Yes, most of them"; yet the farmer, who had lived in the village all his life, couldn't do the same.

Having a large garden meant we were in an ideal position to hold the annual church/village fete with all the usual stalls, skittles, side-shows and teas served from the house. It was a social occasion to bring the village together and was well supported by the other villages around. One farmer did comment to me that it would have been much easier for him to donate x amount than to spend so much time moving tables and chairs from the village hall with his tractor and trailer! I felt the social aspect of a fete to be an important part of village life as it brought everyone together, whether church members or not.

Our farming neighbour came to our rescue one Sunday morning. I had returned home with the children while my husband went on to take yet another service only to find that 'something' was jumping around in the rabbit/guinea pig cage on the lawn. Fred, the guinea pig, was obviously dead and the rabbits were very distressed. They were still in the run so we let them out while the unknown assailant remained shut in the hutch. We then phoned our neighbour who arrived with his gun and shot the offending mink which had, presumably, come from the river two fields away. Sunday lunch was not enjoyed that day! Our son then decided that the rabbits should be sold the next day at a nearby market in case we had another unwanted visitor.

On another Sunday we came out of church to find a film crew together with a number of celebrities performing in the village. Whilst watching we realised that they were filming for "The Two Ronnies". When we eventually saw the series on screen our filming had been cut to just a few minutes and we were able to recognise other local areas where filming had taken place. Such a shame that they didn't need any extras!

We were fortunate to have a very good local primary school which even had a solar heated swimming pool. Our children learned to swim, enjoyed the sports facilities and had a first-class primary school education. It horrifies me now to think we used to let them cycle the one and a half miles to school by themselves!

During our stay it was decided that we needed new hassocks so the decision was taken to make them ourselves. I had organised a flower arranging demonstration in the Village Hall to raise funds for this project. It was a popular event and the hall was full. At some point during the evening the door swung open and in came the local 'special' constable who proceeded, quite loudly and with no apology whatsoever, to inform us that our cars were parked all facing the wrong way and without any lights, and then he was gone. Even in a cul-de-sac in our sleepy village our "Special" stuck rigidly to the Highway Code!

One of the ladies in a nearby village approached me about joining the Mothers' Union. She had a strong faith and a very persuasive character. I joined MU not really knowing what it was all about except that my mother in Wiltshire had been a member for many years. I soon found myself as Deanery Secretary, and later Rep for Deanery Young Families, Group Leader (twice), Archdeaconry Chairman, Trustee and finally Correspondent for Diocesan Members. I had become hooked!

For many years it was the custom in Anglican churches for members of the congregation to donate money at Easter to buy lilies in memory of a loved one. Instead of just putting the lilies in two brass vases as was the custom I arranged them in what I thought was quite an artistic way cutting the stems to suit the arrangement. Well, this did not go down well with one churchwarden whose face was a picture when he noticed the lilies. He made me feel that I had committed some sort of dreadful crime!

During these years we certainly experienced the extremes of British weather. The on-going summer drought of 1976 reduced our potato crop to golf ball size, and an unusually severe winter stranded the regulars in the local pub where they had to had to spend several nights as guests of the landlord! There were many cars stuck in snow drifts with notes on the windscreen with the owners' details. I remember my husband trudging through deep snow one Sunday morning to the nearest church, just in case anyone had been brave enough to face the elements. And once, after heavy rain, we watched the River Stour rise across the fields as the little bridge, known as Trill Bridge, became submerged beneath the flood.

During the summer of the infamous drought a local builder, who was a boy when the house was built, told us there was a well in the garden and suggested the area where we should search. We experimented with extensive water divining hazel forks but our new found "skills" proved frustratingly unsuccessful. Only later did we find that the builder had been many yards off course when giving his advice. However, I am now pleased to report that the well was subsequently discovered and has since been fully restored.

The Rectory

Sadly our lovely home was eventually sold as the Diocese deemed it too expensive to maintain. Some years later my son and I had the opportunity of returning to look round the house. The new owners had undertaken extensive refurbishments and modernisation and had turned it into an extremely comfortable and "desirable residence". Even so, as often happens with renovations, a lot of the original character and charm had been lost. Nevertheless, our return visit brought back treasured memories of the five halcyon years we were so lucky to have spent in a splendid house in its "glory days".

Cerne Abbas

By Devina Symes

Remnants of the past are here,
Scattered everywhere
In this lush valley
where fragments abound
of days gone by,
And still
near St Augustine's well
on this sacred ground
flowing water and nature reveal
a peace, which can renew and heal.
A peace, which, perhaps
the monks left behind,
before the mysterious giant appeared
to guard the village.
While St Mary's rings out the hour,
And the river Cerne meanders through
to join the Frome on its journey to the sea
just as we – continue on to eternity,
to join those souls, now gone
yet through their legacies, live on
in this very special settlement
this Abbey of Cerne
where, if we dare,
We can touch the land of lost content.

RAF Warmwell Airfield

By Brian Sneddon

Before WW11 as air power increased, and Germany threatened to engulf Europe in war, there was a demand for facilities to enable RAF personnel to train in gunnery and bombing techniques.

Chesil Beach was chosen as the location for an armament practice range, and The Air Ministry announced that it would establish an airfield to service this range near to the village of Crossways, not far from Dorchester.

In spite of local opposition construction began in 1936, and facilities included officers' quarters and mess, a flight shed, and various stores such as an armoury, parachute store, and an aviation fuel facility.

Construction work was still progressing in early 1937 when the first airmen were drafted to No 6 Armament Training Camp, Woodsford, the original name for Warmwell.

The first task for the airmen was to complete their own accommodation, and prepare the camp for operational service.

The accepted date of the opening of Warmwell is May 1st 1937, and on July 10th an Avro Tutor training biplane was the first plane to land, and this date is classed as "The Beginning".

During the following weeks a number of Westland Wallace aircraft arrived for conversion to the task of target towing. In 1937 the Annual Coastal Defence Exercise took place and Avro Ansons, temporarily based here participated. In January 1938 the first of several Flying Training Schools began to arrive, and as the year progressed various RAF and Auxiliary Air Force units arrived for armament practice.

On August 24th1939, Britain mobilised, and the next day No 10 Observer School was established at Warmwell with a wide range of aircraft including Harrows, Overstrands, Sidestrands, Hawker Hinds, Fairey Battles, Seals and Wallaces. On November 1st it was retitled No 10 Bombing and Gunnery School. Six days later The Central Gunnery School was formed at Warmwell.

Construction work during 1939 was speeded up, and two Bellman hangars were erected together with a number of smaller buildings. Needless to say accommodation was severely limited, and tents and billets in surrounding villages were often used. The station continued with its programme of training augmented by coastal patrols carried out by Avro Ansons until the fall of France in May 1940.

Spitfires were dispatched to Warmwell from Middle Wallop using the airfield as a forward base to protect Portland harbour. Because of its pre-war role as an Armament Training School, Warmwell had facilities not normally associated with satellite stations and by the end of the month 609 Squadron were stationed there fulltime. They were later augmented with 152 Squadron Spitfires.

During the summer there were a number of attacks on Portland one leading to the sinking of HMS Foylebank, and in August there was one attack in which the Germans used over

200 aircraft, of which 10 were shot down for the loss of 3 of our aircraft.

In August and September, at the height of The Battle of Britain, attacks were concentrated on RAF Fighter Command airfields, in so that with freedom of the sky, there could be an invasion of The UK. Warmwell was attacked several times, and aircraft from Warmwell were constantly in action, and were credited with 18 kills, 5 probables, and 4 damaged for the loss of 3 of our aircraft (two pilots safe). The German losses were such that Ju87 dive bombers were taken out of the battle.

For the rest of the year many sorties were flown to intercept raiders intent on bombing our aircraft manufacturing locations in the South West, with Yeovil and Bristol being most important, and also protecting Portland naval base.

At the start of 1941 there were several more attacks on Warmwell causing a number of fatalities. By summer the airfield was fully integrated into Fighter Command, and 203, then 234, and later 402 Squadron arrived to take on offensive strikes against targets in Normandy using " Hurribombers", Hurricanes carrying 250, or 500 lb bombs. During this period aircraft from Warmwell were involved in the ill fated Dieppe commando raid.

There were other activities, a Wellington bomber was based there and used to test Barnes Wallis's theory of bouncing bombs, bouncing the prototype across the water in The Fleet Lagoon formed by Chesil Bank.

By 1941 the chances of a successful rescue of an airman from the sea had risen to around 35%, and in August Coastal Command had been given the responsibility of Air Sea Rescue (ASR).Initially a detachment including a Supermarine Walrus amphibians were used. Over time a number of different squadrons operated from here over the period to 1943/4 .

In November 1941, No 10 Group established a Practice Camp at Warmwell for its fighter squadrons to use the two firing ranges at Chesil. A target towing flight was formed using Westland Lysanders, which were also used as spotters for Air Sea Rescue missions.

In March 1942 the Canadian squadron 234, left to be replaced by 175 Squadron, again with Hurricanes.

Later that year the Hurricanes were replaced by 266, and later 257 squadrons of Hawker Typhoons. These aircraft undertook regular patrols along the south coast as a counter to the Luftwaffe's low level tip and run raids made by Fw 190s. At that time the Typhoon was the only RAF fighter capable of matching the German aircraft in speed. The Typhoons stayed until January 1943.

In September 1943 a squadron of Westland Whirlwinds (263)

arrived to share duties with the Typhoon squadrons, and together they started to go on the offensive with strikes on German shipping, sinking five E-boats and an armed trawler. Frequent sweeps over northern France created mayhem among the German land forces.

In March 1944 the RAF handed over the airfield to the USAAF Ninth Air Force equipped with the twin boomed P-38 Lightnings . There were three squadrons 428-430. Initially they provided long range escorts for the Eighth Army Air Force, which consisted mainly of B-17 and B-24 bombers, but as D-Day approached they sought out targets of their own, forward of the beaches. In August after having given cover for the initial stages of the invasion, they moved out to an airfield near Paris. The RAF returned to set up No 14 and 17 Armament Practice Camps which were used by various Typhoon and Spitfire squadrons for the next twelve months.

The camps were closed down in October 1945, and the camp was placed under Care and Maintenance. After being used as a base for demobilisation purposes and a reception centre for RAF families returning from abroad, the airfield was sold in 1950, and returned to agricultural use. In 1973 it was sold to Amey Roadstone and ECC Quarries for them to extract gravel, and the site became like a lunar landscape, when extraction was completed. The site was again sold, this time for development.

In 2014 approval for the development of a holiday resort and nature reserve was given, and work started in 2016 to build up to 1000, houses, lodges and chalets, in an environmental friendly manner. The resort is called SILVERLAKE and its military history has been of paramount importance to the developers.

The logo of Silverlake is a Spitfire , which is echoed by a half-scale wicker Spitfire model on the way into the estate.

The villages on site are all named after pilots including Beaumont, Overton and Wakeling, with further villages in development. All of the facilities at Silverlake are named after aircraft, including the stunning Hurricane Spa. Further on into Silverlake, past fishing lakes, tennis courts, forest playgrounds and trails is Knighton Heath Wood, which has recently become home to a memorial plaque to those who were based at RAF Warmwell, installed by Airfields of Britain Conservation Trust.

Thus although very little of RAF Warmwell now exists, its existence will not be forgotten, neither will the RAF and USAAF personnel who lived and died during the period of 1937-46.

The Devonshire and Dorset Regimental Memorial at the National Memorial Arboretum

By Lt. Col. Geoffrey Nicholls (Retd)

The National Memorial Arboretum (NMA) was opened in May 2001 at Alrewas, near Lichfield in Staffordshire. It was established in an area which had been used extensively for quarrying sand and gravel and initially it was not a particularly attractive place and very liable to flooding. Nonetheless, there were plans to make it the National Centre of Remembrance and as 'a toe in the water' the Devonshire and Dorset Regiment agreed to have three trees planted in memory of The Devons, The Dorsets and The Devon and Dorsets. Those trees are still there, now somewhat larger, and the plaques beside them have recently been re-painted.

In 2003 the Ulster Ash Grove was established within the NMA. A tree was planted in memory of each member of the Armed Forces who had been killed in action during 'The Troubles' in Northern Ireland including six Devon and Dorsets. The Grove has since become well established and is a moving place to visit.

The large, circular, Armed Forces Memorial located in the centre of the NMA site was dedicated in October 2007 by the Archbishop of Canterbury in the presence of Her Majesty The Queen and lists all members of the Armed Forces who have died while serving since the end of the Second World War. But by no means all the memorials have military connections – for instance Dorset Constabulary are represented in an avenue appropriately named 'The Beat'.

From the early days of the NMA, members of the Devonshire and Dorset Regimental Association began to visit and gradually, as more and more memorials were constructed, there was a feeling that maybe the Regiment should have one there in addition to the trees and the names on the Armed Forces Memorial. So it was that a five year project began with the NMA authorities earmarking a very suitable plot – the first genuine step forward.

Subsequently ten artists were identified and approached. The only guideline given to them was that the memorial should represent the Regiment's ethos of 'understated excellence' – but the design was entirely up to them. Their responses were considered and eventually it was agreed that Mrs Vivien Mallock's concept was the most suitable. She had produced a number of bronze statues in the UK and abroad, all of which were of a very high standard and she was clearly enthusiastic about producing a memorial for the Regiment. It was agreed that there should be three life-sized figures of a Devon soldier from WW1, a Devon and Dorset in Northern Ireland and a Dorset from Kohima. Stone plinths as well as an explanatory panel would be produced by Phoenix Marble and Granite Ltd, based near Wimborne.

To enable the project to reach a conclusion there was a need for funds. The Regimental Charity Trustees agreed to find enough from Regimental investments to allow for initial bills to be paid, but there was a clear requirement for fundraising – HRH The Duke of Kent (former Regimental Colonel-in-Chief) was approached to act as project Patron and the two county Lord-Lieutenants as Vice Patrons. All three agreed. The people of Devon and Dorset and their various Councils were very generous and eventually all the bills were paid!

The Memorial

It wasn't until the last week of August 2017 that it all started to come together with the three statues finally being erected on their plinths at the NMA.

The Dorset Regiment Statue and Badge

A pretty intense couple of days involved, not least, a 250-mile journey with the stone and bronze figures on board an 18-ton lorry from Dorset to Staffordshire. Even then it wasn't until just days before the Dedication Ceremony that the final turf was laid and the safety barriers around the site could be taken away.

After years of painstaking preparation, pivotal decisions, detailed staff work, artistic endeavour and comprehensive fundraising, the Regimental Memorial was finally and formally dedicated at 1.00 pm on Sunday 17th September 2017. Hosted by the Chairman of Trustees, General Bryan Dutton, 450 guests were present including the Patron, Vice Patrons and ten Dorset Mayors. Prayers and speeches over, the

Captain Jeremy Archer (Society member and Regimental Trustee) and the Lord-Lieutenant meet HRH The Duke of Kent.

Last Post was sounded, HRH laid a wreath and the spectators departed to the evocative sound of the Regimental March played by former members of the Regimental Band.

A marquee reception followed the service, at which HRH was able to meet many of those present before formally signing the Donor's Book. As people drifted away they were aware that they had been privileged to have attended a truly memorable Regimental event.

Readers will invariably find a visit to the NMA worthwhile. It may be a distance to travel, but the over 300 memorials are many and varied, representing all sorts of organisations. It's a large area to walk around, but there is a 'land train' to make it easier, and there is an outstanding café/restaurant! A very comprehensive website www.thenma.org.uk will assist with planning a trip.

13 Easton Street, Portland

By Susan E. Dean – nee Brown

In 1958 my father Philip Brown announced the family was moving to 13 Easton Street, Portland, a renovation project for him, income potential and a larger home for the growing family. He took my mother, Florence to see the new house. She stood on the ground floor with their baby son in her arms and was able to see blue sky two floors up! I was born there on 24th September, just a few weeks before his death on 7th November 1960. Sadly, Philip never really completed that renovation.

The Weymouth Directory of 1960 lists the Brown family as living at number 11 Easton Street, and Beale & Scott, drapers and Modern Cleaners at number 13 Easton Street.

During the time of the Brown family residence the front door was in the centre, a large solid oak door leading to a passage which went all the way to the door of the one bed-roomed flat at the rear of the plot. I can remember several of the former tenants; Ken and Rosemary Whyman on Naval duties stayed more than once and longer term tenants were two lovely girls from St. Helena, one of whom married another tenant, becoming Mrs. David Hall.

Philip negotiated a lease with a dry-cleaning firm; to the right of the front door was their shop called 'Sam's'. To the left was a sewing machine sales and repairs shop in much smaller premises than the dry cleaners. A partnership of Norman Beggs and David Hall ran this business, my mother Florence Brown working as receptionist for them occasionally.

The three bed-roomed flat above the shops was the Brown family's living quarters, entered from that long passage off the main street via stairs, edged on the left with several very large tanks full of various fish. The bay window on the left was the room of my birth, our 'best' sitting room. It contained my father's piano and our Christmas tree was always placed in that window.

The bay window on the right was our dining/sitting room, where we watched TV and played games. The left hand window on the top floor was the bedroom I shared with my sister, Helen. The right hand top floor window was our parents' bedroom, with a large built-in wardrobe to unsuccessfully hide Christmas presents. The back bedroom was the domain of our brother Paul; through this room it was possible to access the greenhouse which always smelled of geraniums and then to the flat roof, the tar of which was often sticky in summer.

Once all three children were at full-time school Florence joined the Women's Institute (WI). She discovered flower arranging, which she enjoyed tremendously but more importantly she was very good at it! This brush with the WI introduced Florence to Mrs. Chibnall, the wife of a retired Captain. "Are you in, dear Mrs. B?" is how Mrs. Chibnall announced her presence at the bottom of the stairs when she visited. A group called The Friends of St. George's was formed to save the redundant historic church which, if not repaired and cared for, would surely fall down. Florence became secretary of the fund-raising group to repair the damage caused by the lead having been stolen from the roof. Water had entered the stone and the walls were 'weeping'. In October 1971 St George's church became vested in the 'Friends' so the first steps in the long road to save the church had been taken.

Committee meetings for the Friends of the church, WI get-togethers and an almost constant stream of female visitors would be ushered into the best sitting room and served tea and biscuits on the very best china. Among the friends who called were several ladies from the St John Ambulance, whose Portland HQ was at the top of Easton Street. I can remember June Cox and Mrs Strewkesbury, looking so smart in their St. John uniforms.

Soon it was time to sell the family home and move to the house provided by the council for the Warden, number 20 Marshallsay Road, Chickerell. Florence had successfully gained employment after 22 years. 13 Easton Street was purchased by Mr. I.F. Timms, whose estate agency was at 43 Easton Street.

13 Easton Street, pictured at the beginning of this article painted green in the 1990's was for a time a DIY shop, note the dropped pavement in front of Marshall & Sons window; this was the vehicle access to the workshop.

After a change of paint colour, 13 Easton Street became a bed and breakfast, and when that time came to an end the sale particulars show one photograph from inside the house; the lounge which then spanned the width of the house and included both bay windows. But what really caught my eye was a very large fish tank! It would seem that to live at 13 Easton Street you must like indoor fish! It is now 2019 and Whitestone gallery and café [pictured left] has been occupying 13 Easton Street for several years. The dropped pavement has survived the years, it is needed for access to the more recently built housing at the rear of the street.

We once enjoyed coffee in the area that would have been my father's workroom, on the left at the top of the slope. As my sixtieth year approaches, I think how lucky my family has been to have shared so much history with this building.

A Celebration of Colour - Carolyne Kardia - Sculptor and Painter

By Nick Cooper

Inspired by music, dance and movement, artist Carolyne Kardia's paintings celebrate colour, while her contrasting sculpture installations often evolve within their settings. Her two- and three-dimensional art forms co-exist in their architectural space, working together to form a dialogue with one another.

"I believe you must always look left", says artist Carolyne Kardia explaining how she and her husband Peter found their rural Dorset home, in its tranquil setting, some 26 years ago. It's easy to miss the farm track leading to it, at an awkward bend on the main road, so it was quite by chance that they spotted the sale sign for the property. The barn, which quickly became her studio, was extended to provide additional workspace and a permanent gallery for her distinctive, brightly-coloured paintings and contrasting white sculptures

A Sculptor first and foremost, Carolyne initially studied drawing and painting. She went on to specialise in sculpture, first at the former St. Martin's School of Art, then at the Royal College of Art, where she received her MA in 1977. Developing techniques she discovered during her college years, both art forms have evolved to become of similar importance to Carolyne, who finds her work in one medium lends elements to the other.

"I listen to music a lot", she reveals, "and I also like to dance. I think a lot of the shapes, forms and colours come up in my paintings as well. I like to think of the colours "singing", really, while the sculpture's more to do with balance, so you could think about the body and dance".

While her work shares and draws upon the visual, physical and spiritual aspects of dance and movement, it frequently engages the artist in working in a similar way. For her larger paintings, Carolyne will often use the floor, much as a pavement artist might do, moving around and working on them from either end. Similarly, the form, movement and balance present in her sculptures reflect those characteristics required of the artist for their creation.

Highly vibrant colours have not always been a feature of Carolyne's paintings, though, and she originally drew only in black and white: "Then I got this tiny box of colours and they liberated me in a way. I began to think about the physical application of the pastel, because it's quite sticky and you can pound it in. Gradually, I got interested in pure colour and how it "sings" to itself- the idea of the colour having its own impetus and its own energy- so the painting somehow holds that colour and energy with other colours. I think what often happens in painting is that colours get subdued; they are subservient to an idea or to an overall configuration. What I'm trying to do is to get the colours to somehow be pure and "just there"; to work with quite bright, vibrant colours".

"For some paintings I've done recently, I've been using yellow surfaces and getting the colours to pierce through the yellow surface. All the time it seems the colours need to adopt their own characteristics. They can be quite unexpected, in the way I respond to them, or the way they respond to the surface of the canvas. I like to let them challenge me. The paintings are abstracts, so in a sense the colours have an opportunity to live and I want them to be celebratory- to celebrate colour".

In stark contrast to her paintings, Carolyne's sculptures contain no colour at all. Making dramatic use of scale, space, light and shade they are constructed entirely from plaster and are often produced within their final environment. The technique of making each component of a sculpture also relies on critical timing.

Plaster is first carefully poured onto a plastic sheet, forming an abstract shape. With the plaster partly set, but still pliable, the sheet and its plaster puddle are then suspended on a hook and formed and pegged into shape. By separating the plaster from its backing at the right moment, the sculpture is then created by joining together these formed pieces, which individually resemble immense curls or flakes of white chocolate.

"When sculpting, I always work with the natural state materials", says Carolyne. "There's something so pure and magical about the transition of plaster; mixing and pouring it, letting it set and getting this wonderful form. In the way it exists it almost attracts and reflects the light. Plaster can seem a dead material, but it isn't. It picks up the light and colours of its surroundings and dances with the shadows.

There's a purity about it, but it's also quite raw and I like the fact that it's strange. It's able to metamorphose in the space; it changes as the light changes and I like that".

As her installations are usually created in their eventual surroundings, they are often of a somewhat temporary nature, but Carolyne has not been tempted to cast her work. "I think it would kill it if I were to cast in bronze and destroy its qualities", she explains. "It's not that I don't want to keep them. Some pieces have survived for 20 years and one or two still exist publicly. I would like them to exist, but I think this idea of them being fragile and potentially ephemeral being just there; just balanced so

Carolyne Kardia in her Studio

that, if somebody crashed into it, it would be destroyed- in a sense gives you a bodily awareness of their fragility".

Combining delicate appearance with inherent strength, the material also presents the artist with considerable challenges. As the sculpture becomes ever taller, and the tension within it increases, so the risk of its collapse also increases. "With my painting and my sculpture, I'm always trying to push myself to the edge and into the unexpected", says Carolyne.

During her career Carolyne has taught at various Colleges of Art, and to groups in Dorset and in London. As a qualified Art Therapist, she ran therapeutic pottery sessions with patients at the Jules Thorn Day Hospital in London for some 25 years. She also teaches yoga, taking several classes locally each week.

Carolyne exhibits regularly at venues throughout Dorset and beyond, her work has also shown at galleries in London, Manchester, Belgium and Germany. The Max-Pianck-lnstitut in Berlin still displays the plaster installation she made there for her 2002 European exhibition, while her sculpture, Spiration, a complex work based on the DNA Double Helix, was displayed for several years in the Science Wing of Sherborne School.

In spring 2010, Carolyne participated in an exhibition at London's exciting Ambika P3 venue. Curated by husband Peter Kardia, a radical and influential teacher at both St. Martin's and the Royal College of Art during the 60s and 70s, "From Floor to Sky" featured the work of a number of well-known artists, who were among Peter Kardia's former students from those early days. An accompanying book, From Floor to Sky, catalogued and expanded on the exhibition.

Website: www.carolynekardia.co.uk

Butterfly Conservation Dorset

By Robin George

By a fortunate combination of climate and geology, Dorset is one of the best counties in the UK for butterflies, with 46 of the 59 regularly seen species in the UK living in Dorset. This has also made Dorset the home to some of the most enthusiastic and fanatical butterfly experts. One of the earliest of these was J C Dale 1792 - 1872 who lived in Glanvilles Wootton. "I would go through fire and water for insects" he wrote. His huge collection of butterflies and other insects, many long since extinct in this country is now held by Oxford University. More recently, it is fitting that the national charity Butterfly Conservation, which has just celebrated its 50th year, has made its home in Dorset. More than 80 scientists and support workers work in modern offices created from handsome old farm buildings tucked away in East Lulworth near Wareham.

Butterfly Conservation's aim is to save butterflies, moths and our environment. It was established more than 50 years ago by a small group of enthusiastic naturalists. It has grown to a large and well-respected organisation, one of the largest insect conservation charities in the world, with more than 34,000 members and 15,000 volunteers. It is very proud to have Sir David Attenborough as its president. Butterfly Conservation's work can be broadly divided into four strands, Recording, Conservation, Education and Reserves. Every summer Butterfly Conservation runs one of the largest citizen science surveys in the UK, the Big Butterfly Count, in which everyone is encouraged to spend fifteen minutes outside, looking for butterflies. More than 100,000 people took part in last year's survey, counting very nearly a million butterflies.

The national organisation heads a large number of regionally-based volunteer-run branches of the charity, of which the Dorset branch is one of the most long-standing and active. Run entirely by volunteers, the branch arranges a wide selection of events and activities each year, based round the four strands of Butterfly Conservation's work. We have nearly a thousand members in the Dorset branch, most of whom live in Dorset. We are united by our love of butterflies and moths, and our desire to see them thriving.

One of the most important aspects of our work is Recording. Butterflies are valuable indicator species, they are very sensitive to changes in climate and habitat, so keeping track of their numbers from year to year is very important. Arguably the most important aspect of recording is the Transect Walk. If you venture into some of the deepest parts of the Dorset countryside you may come across a person deep in concentration, clipboard in hand, eyes flicking from side to side in search of butterflies. This will be one of our transect walkers, following a standardised method of counting butterflies developed by Dr Ernie Pollard more than 40 years ago. Every week from April to October, a hardy band set out to re-trace the steps of last week's walker, last year's walker, and in some cases the walkers of 40 or so years ago. Their route is divided up into sections, and they count every butterfly seen on the route. Back at home the numbers are entered into the computer and go into a national database where they can be compared with the results from last week, last year or many years ago. In this way we build up a pattern of what to expect, and can get warning when a particular butterfly is not faring as well as it used to, and can try to plan changes to help it. It may be, for example, that over-grazing has reduced the amount of the caterpillar foodplant available, or that under-grazing is allowing larger plants to swamp a particular species. At the national scale, the data is being used to help with the assessment of global warming.

Alners Gorse/Fontmell Down

Our longest standing Dorset transect walks were set up by professionals in the 1970s at Ballard Down, Radipole Lake and Hengistbury Head. However, the first one to be set up by volunteer 'Citizen Scientists' was at Fontmell Down in North Dorset in 1980. Not for the faint-hearted, this walk consists of 14 sections, and takes about 2 1/2 hours to walk, with serious amounts of up and down! It compensates its walker by being situated in one of the most beautiful and butterfly-rich parts of Dorset. Last year, over the 26 weeks of the season, 34 different species were recorded at Fontmell, and a total of 4621 butterflies counted.

For those who cannot manage a walk this long, or who live in other parts of Dorset, there are another 80 or so transect walks, covering the whole county, from Swanage to Shaftesbury, Bournemouth to Beaminster.

We are interested in every butterfly seen in Dorset and collect records of where and when they were seen. Our website, www.dorsetbutterflies.com has a facility to allow you to enter details of any butterflies you see, and we always welcome new records and new recorders.

All our records are held in a database, which currently holds more than a million records, dating back to 1831, and including a Brown Hairstreak from Glanvilles Wootton recorded by J C Dale himself in 1842. In 2018 we added more than 600,000 records to the database. Conservation work tends to take place in the winter, when the work of butterfly counting and recording is replaced by conservation action days. Every year a hardy tribe battles with the Dorset mud and blackthorn and hawthorn scrub to try to create and maintain the habitat the butterflies need. Work parties are hard work, but they are also very enjoyable, usually featuring a big fire and plenty of hot drinks and cake, and sometimes jacket potatoes cooked in the fire. Recent research has emphasised the benefits of volunteering, and of being outside, so the 'Green Gym' has a lot to recommend it.

Lydlinch Common in North Dorset is a key butterfly site, where conservation days take place regularly through the winter. It consists of a mosaic of herb-rich grassland, scrub and woodland with a rich population of butterflies, moths and flowering plants, and is notified as a Site of Special Scientific Interest (SSSI). The Blackmore Vale was once full of this type of land, but agricultural improvement has resulted in considerable loss of this declining resource, and in the Vale it is now largely confined to the Lydlinch area. The site lies on the Oxford Clays and can be very wet for most of the year. This makes for very rapid growth of the plant life, particularly hawthorn and blackthorn. A tricky balance needs to be maintained, retaining enough scrub for the nightingales which nest deep in the bushes, whilst also trying to keep some of the site more open, encouraging the Devils Bit Scabious needed by the Marsh Fritillary, a rare butterfly which also makes Lydlinch Common its home. In recent years, our volunteers' efforts have been strengthened by those of a herd of cattle, who now lightly graze the site from time to time.

Marsh Fritillary

Modern approaches to conservation understand that butterflies do not live in isolation, but need to be able to move around. Small isolated populations are very vulnerable to disease, or changes or losses in the plants they rely on and can decline very suddenly. Landscape-scale conservation tries to provide corridors through which butterflies can move to other suitable areas, leading to greater genetic diversity and a more robust population. With this in mind Butterfly Conservation has joined a project called Back from the Brink with other charities, such as the RSPB and the Bumblebee Conservation Trust to try to save 20 species from extinction, and benefit more than 200 other species at the same time. Here in Dorset we are involved in the Back from the Brink project to try and save the Barberry Carpet Moth. Caterpillars of the Barberry Carpet moth feed on Common Barberry, a shrub which used to be found in hedgerows and woodland edges. Common Barberry was a host for wheat rust fungus, and so was almost eradicated to protect the wheat. New rust-resistant varieties of wheat mean that Common Barberry is no longer a problem, but meanwhile the moths had become extremely scarce. In Dorset a single site remained. The Back from the Brink project is planting more Common Barberry on the remaining site, and in suitable nearby areas, to try and increase the population, and make it less vulnerable. Last winter in Dorset, more than 950 plants were planted and we eagerly await news of whether they are thriving, and how the moths have responded.

Education. Our events team visit many local shows and fairs, such as the Oak Fair at Stock Gaylard, and the Dorset County Show to raise awareness and talk to people about butterflies and moths. They often take last night's moth trap catch, and some interesting caterpillars to attract the children's attention. It seems that most butterfly enthusiasts first became interested as children, so it's vital to involve them wherever possible. They are the butterfly and moth guardians of the future.

Members of the team visit local schools to talk to the children, and school visits to our reserves can be arranged.

Our guided walks, run throughout the summer are nearly always open to all. With an expert leader we visit the most butterfly-friendly parts of the county at a time of year when the most species are likely to be seen. As butterflies have good taste in countryside, this often involves visiting some of the loveliest parts of Dorset.

We also help people who are trying to make their own gardens and land more butterfly-friendly. Our website has a wealth of advice on wildlife gardening, and many of our members have wide experience of which plants to grow and how best to encourage butterflies.

Reserves. We have reserves at Alner's Gorse, near Hazelbury Bryan, Lankham Bottom near Cattistock and Broadcroft on Portland. Visitors are welcome at these reserves where a wide range of Dorset's butterflies and moths can be seen.

The reserve at Alner's Gorse is a well-known hotspot for the hairstreak group of butterflies, as well as being a summer home to the nightingale. If you visit on a hot summer afternoon you may meet the keen photographers who cluster round a tree or shrub with their huge lenses, all trying to get the perfect shot. Look for the areas where the grass has been well-trampled, to give you an indication where the butterflies are likely to be seen. Alner's Gorse is part of the old mosaic of North Dorset commons, and was acquired by Butterfly Conservation in 2005. Since then the reserve has been managed to encourage the spread of the internationally threatened Marsh Fritillary butterfly from nearby sites. Trees were felled and areas opened up to encourage the growth of flowers. A team of ponies helps with the work of keeping the ground open, and this year we are extremely pleased that record numbers of Marsh Fritillaries have been seen at the reserve.

My parents both used to tell me about the clouds of butterflies that they remembered in the fields in their childhoods in the 1930's and 1940's. One of my happiest memories is of taking them to Melbury Down near Compton Abbas when they were both in their seventies and could only just negotiate the stile at the entrance. There, one sunny summer's afternoon when the Marbled Whites and the Dark Green Fritillaries were flying together with the Meadow Browns and the rest of the summer butterflies I was able to show them such clouds again. I hope that one day our great grandchildren will be able to see the same sight, and I believe that supporting Butterfly Conservation is one of the best ways to ensure the future of these beautiful insects that we all love.

White Admiral

We would love to see any readers at our events, and extend a warm invitation to you all. Please do look at our website for latest details of our activities, and more information about what we do, and feel free to get in touch with any questions or comments.

The Society of Dorset Men puts Dorset Year Books Online

The Society of Dorset Men was founded in London in 1904 and each year since, with a few exceptions, it has published the Dorset Year Book. In 2017 the Committee of the Society determined to embark on a programme of digitalisation in order for the Year Books to be available online for researchers and other interested parties.

With the celebrations for the 100th Anniversary of the Armistice in 1918 it was decided to start with the issues which covered the First World War and these were duly launched at the Homecoming Event held in the Corn Exchange, Dorchester, last November. Now the digitalisation of the issues for the Second World War has been completed in time for the 75th Anniversary of D-Day and they have been uploaded to the Society's website (societyofdorsetmen.co.uk).

These Year Books are a treasure trove of articles, poems and photographs which fully support the aims of the Society, stated at its foundation as being 'to foster a love of and pride in the county, its history, culture and traditions.' Those for WWI contain many articles detailing the actions of the Dorset Regiments and the theatres in which they served as well as contributions from such literary luminaries as Thomas Hardy, H Rider Haggard, Jerome K Jerome, Warwick Deeping and H G Wells.

The Society of Dorset Men consists of members worldwide who have connection with the county by birth, descent, marriage or property, and it is actively seeking new members.

Peter Lush at work digitalising the Year Books

Annual subscription is £15.00 and Life membership costs £200.00.

An application form can be downloaded from the website and sent to the Membership Secretary, Peter Lush, who is also co-ordinating the project to digitalise the Year Books for the website.

Thomas Pride VC of Wool

By Alan Brown

This nineteenth century hero has largely been forgotten in Wool but the idea has been put to the Parish Council to honour him with a plaque and this is being considered at the time of writing.

Thomas Pride was born March 29th 1835 in Wool, possibly at Bovington as he is shown on the 1841 census as living there with his father Robert Pride , an agricultural labourer, and his mother Ann. This was some sixty years before the War Department bought Bovington and Wool Heath from the Framptons of Moreton. All Bovington consisted of at that time was the farm and a handful of cottages along the road to Clouds Hill. By 1851 Pride was living in Bindon Lane, Wool.

Bovington Farm (Before the days of the Army)

Thomas joined the Royal Navy and served in the China War between 1857 and 1860. He was serving on board HMS Chesapeake at the time of the 1861 census and in that same year he married Elisa Coombs from Wareham.

In August 1864 Thomas was serving aboard the British Flagship HMS Euryalus, part of a squadron of nine British, five Dutch, and three French warships, and 2000 soldiers that were involved in a two-day battle to open the Shimonoseki Strait, in Japan. On September

6th 1864 at Shimonoseki, Thomas, who was now a Colour Sergeant was the Captain of the After Guard, who, with Colour Sergeant William Seeley, accompanied Midshipman Boyes carrying the Queen's Colour.

The citation reads:- "On 6th September 1864 at Shimonoseki, Japan, Captain of the After Guard Pride was one of the two Colour Sergeants who accompanied Midshipman D G Boyes from HMS Euryalus when they carried the Queen's Colour into action in the capture of the enemy's stockade. They kept the flag flying in spite of the fierce gunfire which killed Colour Sergeant Seeley and severely injured Pride. He and the Midshipman, however, did not falter and were only prevented from going further forward by direct orders from their superior officer".

THOMAS PRIDE VC with thanks to John Richardson for this photograph of his Great Great Grandfather

Both men were presented with the Victoria Cross at Portsmouth on 22nd September 1865. Thomas was discharged from the Navy in 1866. In the 1881 census he was a Toll Collector living in the Tollgate House at Parkstone. Prior to this he lived at Sandford, and in 1891 he was living at St John's Hill, Wareham. He died on July 16th 1893, aged 58, and is buried at All Saints Church, Branksome. His grave is marked with a cross. His V.C. is on display at the National Maritime Museum, Greenwich.

What a story to tell of a very brave man from a remote Bovington farm with Wool Heath as a playground, who went to the China Wars and to Japan, and then back home to Dorset. My thanks go to Mary Brinson, nee Pride, for drawing my attention to her heroic ancestor.

The Untold Story Of Those Who Enabled D-Day to Happen

by John Travell

The 75th Anniversary of the enormous, unprecedented, cross-channel invasion of mainland Europe which took place on D. Day, 6 June 1944, was movingly commemorated in many places across this country and in Europe, as those whose countries and communities were involved, remembered and honoured those who were there. The great main event, held in Portsmouth, was attended by the Queen, the President of the United States and the representatives and heads of state of the many countries which took part. Among all those present, the centre of attention and the undoubted heroes of the occasion were the now elderly and dwindling number of survivors of those who had served in the ships and landed on the beaches of Normandy and taken part in the liberation of Europe. The media coverage was considerable, and BBC and television channels gave a great deal of their time to interviewing the veterans and hearing their individual stories. Our Society member, Christopher Jary, has produced an outstanding new and detailed record of the part the Dorset, Devon and Hampshire regiments played as Montgomery's *D-Day Spearhead Brigade* (which I strongly recommend as one of the best and most readable and authentic accounts of this campaign, and a must for anyone seriously interested in knowing what actually happened on the Normandy beaches that day.) For this book, Christopher gathers personal stories from 83 veterans recounting what they did then, as each hour of that day unrolled, and these contemporary accounts win their own words bring the experiences of those who were there vividly alive.

In *The Times,* the war historian, Max Hastings, wrote, 'For us in 2019 D. Day is a fact, a moment of shared Anglo-American experience that is glorious, in so far as anything about war is glorious.' He sets out the vast scale of the operation; 'British and American planners, almost all civilians in uniform, had performed prodigies of organisation to marshal huge land, sea and air forces...An initial U.S. landing force of 130,000 men would be followed by a further 1.2million men by D.Day+90 days, supported by 137,000 wheeled and semi-tracked vehicles, 4,217 tanks and self propelled guns, and 3,500 artillery pieces. Once ashore, the allied armies would require 26,000 tons of fuel and supplies a day to sustain them, representing 301b per American and 201b per British soldier ...The logisticians brilliantly solved the problems of shipping across the Atlantic and then across the channel everything from tanks and jeeps...together with shells, ration packs, wound dressings, blankets, small arms, chocolate..."

Also in *The Times* the chief of the defence staff, General Sir Nicholas Carter, wrote that all those who took part in the invasion and stormed the beaches 'were only the tip of the national spear. Behind them was a vast enterprise that had been years in the planning...Many of the key planners were civilians drafted into uniform for the war: scientists, mathematicians and professionals. They poured over loading tables and shipping calculations, railway schedules and fuel graphs. They devised organisation and method by which half a million vehicles and more than two million men were transported to France, armed and fed and fuelled and supported through the 11 months of combat which followed.'

The Times included a number of interviews with those who had taken part in the D. Day landings in1944. Among these were two, Frank Mosque, who had been a corporal in the Royal Engineers on Sword Beach, and Joe Cattini, who drove a lorry on to Gold Beach. Of all the interviews I have read and heard, these are the only ones who have mentioned the Beach Masters who met them when they landed and directed them where to go, and talking to others interested in this historic event, I haven't found anyone else who has seen or read an interview with any Beach Master or his Assistants who were present at every part of the landings. Yet with each of the ten infantry brigades that landed on the British and Canadian beaches at Sword, Gold and Juno, there was a Beach Group with a Military Landing Officer and his Assistants who were among the first to land and were required to stay on the beach and direct the troops as they came ashore. Many of the men in these beach groups were among the first to be injured or killed. On Juno beach, Peter Lucas, an Assistant Movements Control Officer, was seriously wounded within minutes of his landing, and was stretchered back on to a landing craft which was being improvised as a hospital ship. The only recognition of the existence of the Beach Masters on D.Day I've come across is the well-known scene in the film "The Longest Day" in which Kenneth More plays the eccentric naval commander Beach Master with the bull dog, who tells Sean Connery to get a move on and get off the beach because the noise is upsetting the dog.

This naval officer was a genuine character and a Movements Control officer. Movements personnel were involved from the very beginning of the planning for D. Day, from immediately after the successful landing of Operation Torch in North Africa in November 1942, and they were drawn from each of the services, Now they are part of the Logistics Corps, but this was not created until well after that war ended. Usually they are thought of as transport personnel, but their role and importance in every battle, and historically, in every war, is much wider than that, and absolutely vital to a successful outcome. But they rarely get mentioned in any account of a battle or campaign, or are noticed for any medals. This year is also the 75th anniversary of the battle of lmphal and Kohima, which was the greatest battle in the Burma campaign, in which the Dorsets were also involved. This was against the largest Japanese army in history which was on the verge of getting through to India, but was stopped at Kohima and from then on the Japanese were in retreat. In his History of the Second World War, Winston Churchill writes to congratulate Lord Louis Mountbatten, the Supreme Commander in South East Asia, and especially praises those who managed to get the 2nd Division of the British Army 'by every means of transport available" several hundred miles across India in less than two weeks to relieve the besieged garrison on the Kohima ridge. But no member of the Movements personnel who achieved this feat is mentioned by name. They are essential, but always anonymous.

My reason for writing this article, and why I am seeking for a proper recognition for all that the Movements people did to make D.Day possible, is because I am the Chaplain to the Joint Services Movement Control Association, now part of the Logistics Corps. How I got involved is a long story, but a friend of mine, who was a member of my church in London, Lieut. Col. Chris Scott , was a Movement Control Officer in Africa and Italy during the War (The politician Dennis Healey was also a Beach Master at Anzio). Chris started the Movement Control History Society and gathered a considerable archive which includes a large file of the original planning documents for D. Day and several thousand records of Movements personnel. The Chris Scott Archive is now housed at the Logistic Corps H.Q. at the Duke of Gloucester Barracks at South Cerney. These valuable records have never been properly researched, although we have tried to bring them to the attention of the War history Departments of several universities in the hope that they might interest some of their Ph.D.students to produce fresh information and insights about D.Day and other battles from these important historical records"

In an article on 'How Movements Controlled Overlord" written for the Movements Control Journal, Chris explained how the planning for D.Day began in November, 1942, immediately following the successful launch of Operation Torch in North Africa. In April that year, the War Office had set up Operational Planning for a large assault landing and this called for the full-time and exclusive efforts of a Movements staff. A series of 'recces' for suitable 'hard' landing beaches and ports had been undertaken. It was evident that a landing across the channel or the North sea would be much more difficult than the successful landings in Sicily and North Africa. By contrast to the tideless Mediterranean, 'the sea around England had a tide range of 24 feet, deep water rarely found close in, narrow access roads and lanes, with a serpentine coastline, resulting in 24 embarkation points from Yarmouth to Milford Haven - a coastline extending to over one thousand miles.' Behind every embarkation point there was a Concentration Area, a Marshalling Area and an Embarkation Camp. When Montgomery returned from Africa he then doubled the size of the original D.Day force which meant a much greater number of ships and landing craft were needed.

Lt. Cdr Chris & Gerry Scott at the unveiling of the Italy Star Association Memorial at the National Memorial Arboretum - September 2016

A Movements Control department of 18 officers and 30 other ranks, under the command of Lt. Col. (later Brigadier) Tom Collins was formed in April 1944 to co-ordinate and keep watch on the movement of personnel. On the first three tides it was planned to land 130,000 men and 20,000 vehicles. Because the Assault and Follow - Up units had to be loaded simultaneously, there was a major problem with the vehicles which had to be loaded into over 1,000 different ships and craft.

Brigadier Collins wrote his own personal account of all that was involved in moving the Assault Force and the Build Up. Chris says Collin's account 'gives a vivid insight into the many variable factors involved in the planning of every move'. At each of the staging points, the embarkation process had Movement Control personnel checking that briefing and tasks had been properly carried out, and that units boarded the vessels they were meant to be on. Large numbers of Movers were recruited from the Royal Engineers and the Royal Artillery to man the many Embarkation ports. By D.Day+30 Movements had embarked over 1million men and 100,000 vehicles on the British Sector and as many again on the American, from Southampton westwards.

The work of Movements and those putting together the plans for D.Day was every bit as vital and top secret as those employed at the top secret establishment at Bletchley Park. The Movements personnel were based in very cramped quarters at Fort Southwick, near Portsmouth, and had none of the computers which were available to help those at Bletchley, The Movements brief was 'that they were there to meet the needs of the "far shore." Priorities were arranged according to the requirements of the campaign Commanders. All the details for every embarkation point had to be recorded on a massive card index, which grew exponentially as priority lists arrived from overseas and Force Landing Forecasts and Force Movements Tables were made. But frequent changes in priorities and uncertain shipping movements made forecasting almost impossible, and the unforeseeable, unseasonable four day storm which collapsed the American Mulberry harbour doubled the amount of traffic on the British Mulberry. This storm caused havoc with the Build Up of Stores: ammunition, petrol, arms and equipment, as well as post and NAAFI supplies, which the Movements staff from the War Office through to the roadheads and beach landing places were responsible for. The slower turnaround time of ships and craft also slowed up the pace of delivery, and it was August before a satisfactory balance was achieved.

A Movements Advance party was landed in Normandy on D.Day+1, and the Main party two days later. These were based at Banville, a small village two miles from the Gold and Juno boundary, and then, on D.Day+12, the Rear party arrived which included women of the ATS. The records for the stores arriving and passing on through Sword Beach during the first three days were destroyed by enemy action, so there is hardly any documentation available from the Movers who were at work on the beaches in those crucial first days of the invasion. But as Chris Scott writes, "The Movements staff at the War Office, with all the multitude of Movers engaged in embarkation in England, the staff at 2nd Army and 21 Army Group with their "eyes and ears" in the Beach Maintenance Areas and along the L. of C. [line of command] thousands of Movers, were all in the picture, and MOVCO [Movement Control] literally set the wheels in motion in constant struggle to ensure that Formation requirements were met in the right place at the right time.' Which was in the height of battle, from the very beginning to the end of the whole campaign.

Harry Paye - The Old Pirate of Poole

By Kay Ennals MBE

Who was this privateer smuggler who rained havoc around the southern shores of Britain and even in Spanish and more distant seas? He was an infamous raider who would plunder any ship he thought worthy of fighting in order to seize its cargo. He did this with determination and most often with violence.

This was Harry Paye. He was born in Poole in 1360 where he quickly learnt seafaring knowledge from his family and friends. Although they were not rich they managed to live well by bartering and smuggling. Being in Poole it was easy for them to use small boats for transporting their contraband.

Harry grew up in this environment. He could put to sea, make sail, plough the waves and even navigate. His aim was to have his own ship. With this in mind he made connection with those who knew when and where they could sell off their smuggled wares. This was mostly in the small villages within a few miles along the coast from Poole. Swyre and Burton Bradstock were key landing places. Customs officers were of course keen to catch those trading off their plunder but there were known stretches of coastline that remained unguarded. Harry and his friends took advantage of these free landings, as did the local inhabitants who were pleased to receive and pay for the goods offered.

Soon Harry had command of his own ship with a full crew. He grew bolder by setting out to sea along the coasts of France and Spain where he encountered larger ships and engaged them in fight to gain their spoils. He became feared as a most infamous raider. His plundering and pirating continued and often he would be fighting Spanish and French fleets which he had come to regards as the enemy.

A Ship like Harry's

In time Harry became patriotic and would fight for his "Country and Crown", and he became such a nuisance in the Channel that continental royalty were becoming involved.

In 1406 the kings of France and Spain became infuriated by the havoc Paye was causing amongst their fleets. They joined forces and decided to get rid of Harry, his ship and his crew, and they raised an expedition to follow him to Poole with orders to find and kill Harry.

The expedition found Harry's home but the pirate was not to be seen. He'd been warned of their coming and had escaped, but they killed his brother and some of the local people,and they eventually burned down a lot of the town!

On his return, when he discovered the carnage and the killing of his brother, Harry sought revenge. He rallied several ships and with his own he sailed out to find the French and Spanish fleets. He found them and he and his companions sailed broadside along the enemy ships engaging them and demanding their goods. The fighting was intense and later Paye and his flotilla returned to Poole with the spoils of over 120 Spanish and French ships, including one laden with wine. So Harry invited his fellow citizens to drink the wine with him as compensation for the damage they had suffered from the Spaniards and the French!

After much celebration Harry was duly appreciated in the hearts and minds of the townsfolk of Poole and became a significant part of the town's history. He was known as "The Old Pirate" and has become something of a legend. In the early 15th Century he was made a Commander of the Cinque Ports Fleet,and he led this fleet in the name of the King! He died in 1419 but each year in June "Harry Paye Day" is organised along Poole Quay by he "Pirates of Poole". In this way Harry Paye is remembered as one of Dorset's most colourful characters.

The Old Pirate

Dorset's Rare Resident – The Wild Service Tree

By David Downton

I had previously visited the natural burial ground at Higher Ground Meadow, Corsecombe, to attend funerals within it's beautiful setting, and pay respect to former friends and relatives interred there. However, on a balmy May afternoon last year I was there for a different purpose.

Mrs Joanna Vassie, and her husband Peter own and care for the Meadow. They took me to Ashmore, one of the woodland sites therein, to choose a plot and select a native British tree. At the foot of this tree, my ashes will eventually be buried. Higher Ground Meadow is a conservation area where only native plants and trees are allowed to flourish. Walking along grass paths adjoining the lush meadows we saw dark blue heavily scented English Bluebells, the Early Purple Orchid, Yellow Rattle, field Forget-me-nots and a variety of other English wild flowers. A host of subtle coloured meadow grasses swayed in the warm breeze, looking over and protecting the flowers.

This meadowland is untouched, except in autumn when, after the flowers and grasses have seeded, the farm sheep are allowed to crop grass and fertilise the land.

Together we looked at a variety of native trees already established on plots and, being a keen gardener, I enquired about leaf colour, bark texture, flowers and fruits. But above all I asked about the ability of the tree to flourish in meadowland and later to become part of a small copse. Eventually, Mrs Vaisse showed me a flourishing tree which had leaves similar to the English Maple and a distinguished bark. There was a smaller companion nearby blooming creamy white flowers. It was the "Wild Service Tree", of which I had no knowledge.

The Wild Service Tree

So I decided to choose this tree to look over me, because it is elegant, mysterious and as a rare species, I felt it needs to be re-established in our county and country .

When I returned home I began researching the origins and attributes of the tree, and little did I know what interesting facts I would discover.........

It's certainly an old tree and is thought to have entered Britain from the Continent after the last Ice Age, that's some 10,000 years ago. During the Neolithic Age it was a staple, and was popular well into the nineteenth century.

Archaeologists discovered Wild Service charcoal during excavations at the Durotrigean Iron Age hill fort of Maiden Castle. It is uncommon and particularly rare in this part of the country, but more concentrated in the Southern Weald. Although usually a small tree, it thrives and grows larger in deep rich soil continuously supplied with water, but also tolerates dry soils. In autumn its beautiful bright red and copper leaves are among the first to turn and from a distance it can be mistaken for an Acer.

Research records of distribution throughout Britain suggest it grows best in clay or lime soils, although better in some varieties of clay and lime than others. It is rare for a variety of reasons, and being light demanding, only thrives where competitors for light and space are sparse. Therefore, this tree seldom occurs in large densities, more usually as individuals or in groups of less than ten. Dr Oliver Rackham writing in his absorbing book "Trees and Woodlands of the British Landscape " identifies the Wild Service Tree as one of a group of plants who have found it difficult to colonise new sites, but who can survive indefinitely in existing sites .He thinks the reason for this may be climatic changes, preventing them from setting seed. The tree often fails to produce flowers and fruit because it requires a warm climate,which is a problem in Britain where temperatures are often too low for seed to ripen. Therefore it relies on the"back up "method of propagation by producing suckers. Dr

"Chequers" - The Fruit of the Tree

Rackham also believes another reason may be changes in woodland structure, where woods have been discontinuous for centuries, and plants are" unable to move in small leaps through continuous forest .but have to jump across farmland to reach new sites."
That said, the Wild Service tree is the most tolerant of the genus in Britain and is more closely associated with ancient woodland sites than any other species, but continues to decline throughout Britain and Europe
"Service" is an unusual name for a tree and several authorities have suggested that "Service" is a loose translation of the Roman word for beer, "cerevisia".

It was also valued from those times for a medicinal reason, as the species name "torminalis " means in Latin "helpful for colic "Parts from the tree have also proved useful for patients with diabetes and it is one of the twenty most frequently used medicinal plants where it grows in Turkey. In our own times an aqueous bark extract is being used for stomach ache and ulcer treatment.

Richard Mabey writing in "Flora Britannia" argues that "Service" come from the Anglo-Saxon word Syfre which translates as "clean, pure, chaste, sober, not giving way to appetite or passion, abstinent, temperate and circumspect" I grow fonder of my tree the more I discover!

The fruit of the Wild Service is known as "Chequers" which, when ripened, taste like dates and in former times was sold in markets and given to children as sweets . It's well documented that this fruit was used to flavour beer, before hops were introduced, and to make wine. Richard Mabey records that many Public Houses have Wild Service trees in their gardens and when it was safer to drink beer than water, and home brewing was fashionable, brewers tended to use whatever was available .

I thought of the former public house in Dorchester called "The Chequers" where we thought the name derived from customers playing "chequers" (draughts) during their sojourn. Maybe not . These fruits are versatile and used to make a drink called "Ratafia", a fruit or fortified wine-based alcoholic beverage which was popular where the tree grew on the Continent, in wine growing regions .The drink was usually produced from secret recipes passed down through families or small communities. It is one of the most ancient and traditional beverages. Another suggestion why some public houses are called "Chequers", centres around the coat of arms of the local landowners, where the "Chequy Field" on the shield is an area divided into small alternative squares in two colours.

The Prime Minister's country residence at Chequers has Service trees growing in the garden and the coat of arms of a former owner has a chequered design on his heraldic shield.

Wild Service Tree wood is one of the most valuable hardwoods in Europe, and I was privileged recently to handle a small piece, when Robert Simpson ,a friend and master wood-craftsman discovered a rare piece in his extensive wood collection. It has the density of teak, a fine grain and resilient strength when bent. Traditionally, it was used to make screws for wine presses, fine furniture, musical and measuring instruments and its decorative veneer is highly valued. Peter Thomas, writing in The Journal of Ecology, tells us that, at The Paris World Exhibition of 1900, the yellowy red wood of the Wild Service Tree was voted the most beautiful wood in the world.

In 2015 the Dept. of Food Technology at Zagreb University undertook an extensive study of the bark, fruit and seeds of Sorbus Domestica, a relative of the Wild Service . Their conclusions indicated that the bark could be used as a good source of calcium, zinc, iron and phenols, while the seeds provided potash, magnesium, iron and zinc. The outer layer of the fruit was a large source of phenols and flavonoids. It's quite probable that the Wild Service Tree relation could also possess these attributes. Their scientists postulated that parts of this tree could be used as excellent sources of mineral elements and antioxidants vital to our diet.

I am glad that I have chosen this multi-talented tree to be my companion in future years, and hope the genus thrives to enhance the wonderful ecology of Dorset and our country.

Sources

- *"Biological Flora of The British Isles"; Sorbus torminalis- journal of Ecclogy 105 (6) August 2017. P. A. Thomas*
- *The distribution of the Wild Service Tree - Sorbus torminalis (L) Cranttz in "The British Isles" P.Roper*
- *Salisbury E.J and Jane.F.W "charcoals from Maiden Castle and their significance in relation to vegetation and climate conditions in prehistoric times" J of Ecology 20-310-325*
- *Trees and woodlands of the British landscape – Oliver Rackham Dent 2006*
- *Kulturs " Medicinal plants used in Kirklareli province (Turkey J.Ethnopharmacology.2007;111*
- *"Characterisation of Sorbus Domestica L Bark, Fruits and seeds: Nutrient Composition and Antioxidant Activity " Food Technol Biotechnol Dec 2015 53(4)453-471 University of Zagreb*
- *Flora Britannica- Richard Mabey Chatto & Windus/ Sinclair Steverson 1996*
- *"Quaint signs of old inns "Monsone – Fitzjohn G.J.L 1926 London. Herbert Jenkins*

Mrs. Livermore

By David Barnes

She arrived in the spring of 1919 taking up residence in a small one bedroom thatched cottage at the south east end of the village. She purchased the cottage for eighty pounds in the name of Gladys Livermore. In her early twenties, little was known of her former life. She eased herself into the village but because of her shy and reclusive nature she never became one of them. Being a stranger and making no attempt to integrate, she was considered by nearly everyone as strange and unapproachable and so in the early years she was mostly ignored until it became a habit from which the village never recovered.

No-one considered her to be lonely. No-one enquired as to why she was so reclusive. If just one person had called to enquire as to her wellbeing and invited her to their home then her whole life might have turned out different. But in the 1920s and early 30s life was hard. They were the years of the great depression when looking out to one's own family took up most of everyone's time. These were the days of hunger, deprivation and poverty. One other thing that set her apart was she always had enough to live on and so the belief grew that she had a small family inheritance which paid for her basic needs. For more than forty years she added to her income by teaching the piano, playing the organ for the occasional wedding and also for the village choir when the usual organist was unavailable.

Apart from these activities her only other involvement in village life was attending the annual memorial service for the men who lost their lives in the Great War. She went neither to chapel nor church, was never approached to join the WI and shunned by the village children. The grown-ups believed her to be a spinster but no one ever asked. She made no real friends, no one called by.

Because of her reclusive nature she became known to the locals as the lady from Brookside, the name of her cottage. Her life revolved round her home and small garden that included a number of ancient fruit trees from which a local man occasionally took cuttings for grafting. He never entered the cottage but she always gave him a glass of fresh juice which he supped in the garden. His wife picked the apples and in return she baked an occasional apple pie for the lady.

A narrow verge brimming over with a variety of wild and cultivated flowers separated her cottage from the road. Photographers, both amateur and professional keen to record a vision of village life as it was in the early part of the twentieth century were constantly taking photographs. Miss Livermore always declined their request for her to be part of the panorama.

In April 1948 following the winter of the big snow, the mother of five who picked the apples sent her youngest child, a nine year old boy, to help clear a path from her door to the road. The lady gave him sixpence. The boy thanked her, the first time he had ever spoken to her. More than a decade would pass before he did so again. He gave the sixpence to his mother who sent him to the village shop for a beef bone which didn't need coupons. With the bone and a few dumplings she made a stew with which to feed a family of six. Eleven years later on a Saturday evening July 1959, the boy, now a young man and home on leave from the RAF, was preparing to go out with friends when there was a knock on the door. Being alone in the house he opened up. A girl of about ten handed him an envelope and ran off. He knew the child.

He closed the door, sat down at the kitchen table and slit the envelope open to reveal a hand written note folded in two. He noted the neatness of the handwriting and also the quality of the note-paper and was impressed. He began to read: "Dear David, when your mother came to inspect the apple trees for bugs she told me you would be home on leave for two weeks from Thursday. Would you be kind enough to visit me this evening at six thirty, I have a need of your help. Sincerely: Gladys Livermore.

He remembered the sixpence and decided to call on her before meeting up with his friends wondering about the request she was going to make. Her cottage was half a mile away, he walked.

She greeted him at the door: "Hello David, how kind of you, please come in, it has been a long time."

"Hello Miss Livermore I have twelve more days of leave so anything I can do I am more than willing."

It was the first time he had been in the cottage and was immediately struck by the timelessness of both the furnishing and the lay-out. It was like being transported back to the 1900s.

"Thank you David and it's Mrs. although I suspect you are the first person in the village to know that. I was married before I came to Thursford.

Sadly Edward was killed in France in 1917. He was a lieutenant in the county regiment. We married in May of that year, he embarked two weeks later and died in early June. That's a photograph of him taken before embarkation. Due to financial constraints I had to move away from our old home that is why I came here.

"Now before I am too old I would like you to accompany me to London to visit his grave, I thought Tuesday morning if that would suit. I have never made the journey before but I feel a desperate need to make the pilgrimage before it is too late. I will pay all expenses my only request is you wear your RAF uniform."

And so it was that on the following Tuesday David, in best blue and with his new pilot officer's rings on his sleeves, boarded the 8.29 from the local town to Liverpool Street accompanied by a sixty two old lady recently revealed as a WW1 widow. They travelled first class.

The journey was uneventful and although he didn't ask, David wondered where her late husband was buried. On arrival at Liverpool Street they boarded a taxi which took them to the doors of Westminster Abbey. Mrs. Livermore took her young escort's arm and together they strolled down the nave until they came to the Tomb of the Unknown Warrior.

She stopped, let go of his arm and from her coat pocket she took a single red poppy picked that very morning from her cottage garden and preserved in a handful of damp moss wrapped in grease proof paper. She stepped forward and against all the rules and in spite of the number of people standing by the tomb she knelt, placed the poppy on the floor by the rail and said a short prayer.

A guide approached intent on asking her to pick up the flower but David intervened and told him he would remove the poppy himself as soon as she was finished. After less than a minute she stood, bowed to the grave, took David's arm and exited the building. David left the poppy to the guide. Outside the abbey David hailed a taxi directing the driver to Liverpool Street Station where they boarded the one thirty five for home. On the return journey Mrs. Livermore told David her story: "I have been alone for over forty years and have wept every night since I received the telegram informing me of Edward's death in 1917. It simply said: Missing presumed dead.

"I wouldn't wish my lifelong loneliness on anyone. I miss him today as much as I missed him the morning he went away. The hardest thing was not being able to say goodbye. The photograph of him in civilian clothes on the sideboard along with our single wedding photograph, are my only tangible memories of him. I loved him deeply David, I still do. To me he is still the twenty four year old young man I fell in love with all those years ago.

"You may think me a silly old woman travelling all the way to London to visit his burial place but I felt a desperate need to do so and when I learned you were home on leave I knew I could ask you to accompany me."

David paused then gently asked, "How do you know it is Edward who is buried in the Unknown Warrior's Tomb?"

"I have seen photographs and heard stories of women and children searching through the graveyards of Belgium and France hoping to find amongst the millions of crosses and memorial stones, the final resting place of their loved one. I don't have to do that David because like millions of women throughout the land I know it is my Edward who is buried in Westminster Abbey. I know it is him and the knowing has made my life bearable and a little less lonely."

Susan's Ashes

By David Barnes

Sitting by the river I feel as close to her as I had ever been. It was our favourite spot through early spring to late autumn. We would pack a few sandwiches, a flask of coffee, two foldaway chairs, a blanket, a cushion and a book each. I would also take the daily paper. It was only a few yards from a pull-in along a rarely used country lane a mile or so from our home. The meadow where a few cows grazed was flat enough to walk right up to the water's-edge; our small piece of heaven in an otherwise turbulent world.

When my eldest daughter walked with me and asked why I still came here to sit alone I told her it was to remember, she didn't ask again. The truth however is somewhat more involved; those who have lost a soul-mate will understand better than most.

Fifty nine years we had been married when suddenly she wasn't there. There was no long illness, nothing to prepare me: one summer morning she didn't wake up. Eighty one she was and looked no different to me than the day we met. The children and grandchildren took over, everything was arranged and five weeks later a man presented me with a small jug containing her ashes, an urn he called it. I remember thinking it wasn't much but he had already explained to me that the human body was mostly water. I didn't argue with him but I knew Susan was more than water, much more and I didn't like the stopper so I replaced it with an old cork from Susan's box of odds.

I placed the urn on a shelf and told the family that come autumn we would scatter the ashes on top of the hill and let the wind take her where it chose. She would have liked that I thought; and that's what we did.

One evening when the wind was blowing toward the sea we released her from the urn and watched as she winged her way across the lonely eastern sky, well most of her. For on that early autumn evening two years ago, I cheated. The previous morning I had pulled the cork on the urn and shook a few flakes of her ashes into an old biscuit tin. The afternoon following the ceremony on the hill, I put on my old army great-coat she had bought for me in a charity shop, took the tin to our favourite spot by the river and buried it beneath the willow tree where the kingfisher sat silently scanning the meandering stream. I buried it deep so that come flood and high water, there it would remain safe and secure. And that's why I come here, not every day but three or four times a week just to be with her; the other days I spend remembering our life together.

Lonely? You don't know lonely until it happens and when it does it's the worst pain imaginable. There is no cure, no antidote, no one day is better than another. It is ever present, controlling every conscious hour. You wake up with it; eat your meals with it, spend the day with it, go to bed with it, live with it, sleep with it: lonely.

An empty chair, no smile, no glance across a room, no sound, nothing. Those who tell you the pain will ease have not been there. It will not ease, it does not get better. But, being close to her, to an old biscuit tin containing some of her ashes buried beside the river; that helps. As does the kingfisher, the heron, the egrets and the ever present swans. The lightning dace, the sedate perch the mud hugging chubb and the swooping swallows remind me that although nothing is forever, life itself continues.

The kingfisher and the heron are probably the fifth generation of the birds we watched together those many years ago now feeding on the descendants of the original dace while our own great grand-children are at this moment running around the playground of the local village school. On a quiet spring afternoon I can hear them from our garden.

Maybe this evening they will visit and in the face of the youngest girl I will see her again and for a short time the loneliness will abate and I will feel alive again. There are better moments there are, and those are the ones I must cherish.

Heart of Stone

Joanna Ashwanden

Land of stone, land of stone, turned inside out for the heart of stone
taken, transplanted, built into St. Paul's Cathedral, The Palace of Westminster,
The Tower of London, Buckingham Palace, The Cenotaph

We are glad of the strong white stone shaped into the teeth of the earth
but we mourn for it too, for the scars left behind
branched now by buddleia and kissed by silver studded butterflies
shining in the sun

The hollow heart of Portland is a grave itself
for the gravestones of our uncountable war dead

Quarries for the building stone, connected forever
to the buildings which rose from them all joined together to our heart of stone

The Dorset Year Book

(Over recent years in each edition we have carried a feature "Our Year Book 100 Years Ago" compiled by The Rev Dr John Travell, our Chaplain and Historian. However, for a short period in the early 1920s the Year Book covered two years at a time and the feature for 1919-1920 was published in last year's book. So, for this year John has chosen to feature his article on the history of the Year Book as published in his recent Illustrated History of the Society. Ed.)

For those who had left Dorset to live overseas, the Society's Year Book was a welcome and much appreciated reminder of where they had come from. Some of them had been away from Dorset for a very many years and had extraordinary stories to tell. The 1915/16 year book reported the death in Sydney in August 1915, of Mrs. Joseph Kemp who had been born in Poole in 1817. She had emigrated to Australia with her husband in 1854, a journey which took 120 days. "Up to a few days of her decease…she could relate the starting of the railway in England and New South Wales, the old method of open voting in elections, the passing of the Reform Bill, the window tax, the corn laws, anti-slavery agitation etc… She was enthusiastic about Mr. Henniker Heaton's scheme for penny postage throughout the world. She remembered that it cost ninepence to send a letter from Poole to London." Another emigrant was Henry Facet Hurst, who had been born in Blandford in 1833. When he set sail for Australia in 1852, the ship stopped at Liverpool because the owners could not afford to continue the journey. The passengers then took over the ship themselves and continued on their way, taking six months to arrive at their destination. Hurst settled as a successful farmer, until his home was invaded by a notorious bushranger called Burke. In a fight to defend himself and his family, Hurst managed to defeat and capture the thief who was arrested, but sadly, Hurst died of the wounds he had received in the fight.

But the special appeal of the Year Book for those overseas, who eagerly welcomed the arrival of each issue, was in all that they could read in it about the county and the places they had come from and fondly remembered. The Society's President, Sir Frederick Treves, had travelled throughout Dorset in order to research for his book The Highways and Byways of Dorset which was published in 1906. He took nearly two thousand photographs of the towns, villages, and scenery all over the county, and he then gave these to the Editor of the Year Book, Newman Flower. So every Year Book was full of pictures of places which were very little changed from how they were remembered by those who had left them many years before.

How much receiving the Year Book meant to those in remote places overseas is shown by a letter to the Editor, dated December 12th. 1948, from Mrs. Gladys M. Stickland, with the address, c/o London Mission, Tientsin 1, N. China. Mrs. Stickland wrote: "Perhaps you and some of your co-workers on the Dorset Year Book would like to know how one copy of the 47-48 number reached its destination." She went on to explain that for eighteen months, she and two others from Britain had been in communist China carrying out medical missionary work. their mail from home arrived regularly at Tientsin, some ninety miles away and in order to receive it they depended on Chinese small traders who travelled to and fro to bring it to them. In September she had set out to go to Tientsin herself, intending to pick up the mail and also some hospital and household supplies. She describes the journey with a Chinese companion through fields of sunflowers and floodplains until they arrived at Tientsin. Having collected her supplies she then went to start the first forty miles of her return journey by train. Her journey was delayed and interrupted by officials frequently making her open all her bags for inspection "having everything dragged out and examined to see if it was what I said it was." After the third inspection she was ordered to go to a nearby village to see a V.I.P. He sent her back in an open railway truck to Tientsin. She spent two weeks there vainly trying to get a military permit, but without success, so she set out again without one. This time she managed to make it to the border "but a mean little man in uniform…collected my fountain pen, hand torch, my little case of personal medicines containing my pet eye and nose drops etc. He also collected my parcel of Chinese books." Luckily he was not interested in her mail bag which she managed to keep intact until October when she arrived back at her mission station. "Amongst my own mail was the Dorset Year Book. It has been much enjoyed by the three of us here, one a Welsh woman, the other an English doctor born in Madagascar, and myself plain Darset. The book will be re-read many times…Many, many thanks for such a splendid issue.. the farther away I am from Dorset the more I value every link…Yours very sincerely, Gladys M. Stickland."

(1949/50 Y.B. p.166-8.)

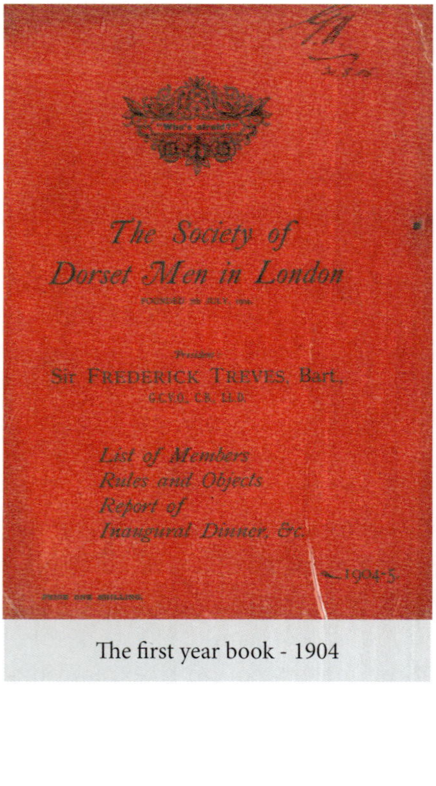

The first year book - 1904

Phone (01258) 820216

Tess' Cottage
Marnhull
STURMINSTER NEWTON
Dorset DT10 1NH

Mr Gordon Hine
Secretary, The Society of Dorset Men
Mortier House
New Road
SHAFTESBURY
Dorset SP7 8QL

4th December 1999

Dear Mr Hine

REPUBLICATION OF 1924 YEAR-BOOK COVER

Further to our telephone conversation earlier today, this is by way of a courtesy 'thank you' for your verbal agreement to the republication of the cover of the 1924 Dorset Year-Book. I hope to include it as part of an item for possible inclusion in a forthcoming 'millennium supplement' to The Marnhull Book, with which you are familiar.

As I told you, the cover of your publication, which shows a Marnhull cottage thought to be the setting for the family home in Hardy's Tess of the D'Urbervilles, adds considerably to the debate since it can by incontrovertibly dated and, most importantly, was published four years before Hardy's death -- and in the prestigious publication of a society of which Hardy himself had been a past president.

I am indebted to the sharp eyes of Dr James Gibson, a Vice-President of the Thomas Hardy Society, for bringing this connection to my attention. In due course I hope to be able to offer a copy of all of the material which I have collected with regard to this fascinating old building to both the Dorset County Record Office and the Dorset County Museum photo library.

Finally, I do hope you understood my reluctance to produce a piece for inclusion in your current journal. We are trying desperately to walk the fine line between being hospitable to the legions of Hardy enthusiasts who seek us out and not turning our private residence into a tourist venue, for which it is singularly unsuited -- we do not wish to draw any more public attention to ourselves than is absolutely necessary!

Thank you again for your help and kindness.

Yours sincerely

Christopher Edwards

Copy to Dr James Gibson

"WHO'S A-FEÄR'D?"

The DORSET YEAR-BOOK

Published by THE SOCIETY OF DORSET MEN IN LONDON.

20th Year of Issue. 1924.

Photo by E. J. Trowbridge

Old Cottage at Barton, Marnhull, Dorset,
Reputed to have been the home at "Marlott" of Tess of the D'Urbervilles.

Copies of this Year-Book, price 2/6 (by Post 3/-), can be obtained from the Hon. Secretary, Mr. William Watkins, 274, Gresham House, Old Broad Street, London, E.C. 2.

An Illustrated History of the Society of Dorset Men

The opposite page is a facsimile of the front cover of the History of our Society compiled by The Rev. Dr. John Travell, our Chaplain and Historian.

This 98-page perfect-bound softback is a comprehensive account of the shape and activities of our Society dating back to its inception in London in 1904.

It's a very good read and every member should have a copy!

John holds a stock of the book and will be pleased to post to you upon receipt of £9 per copy, including post & packing.

Cheques payable to:
The Society of Dorset Men.
Post to: **Rev. Dr. John Travell,**
44 Cornwall Road,
Dorchester DT1 1RY

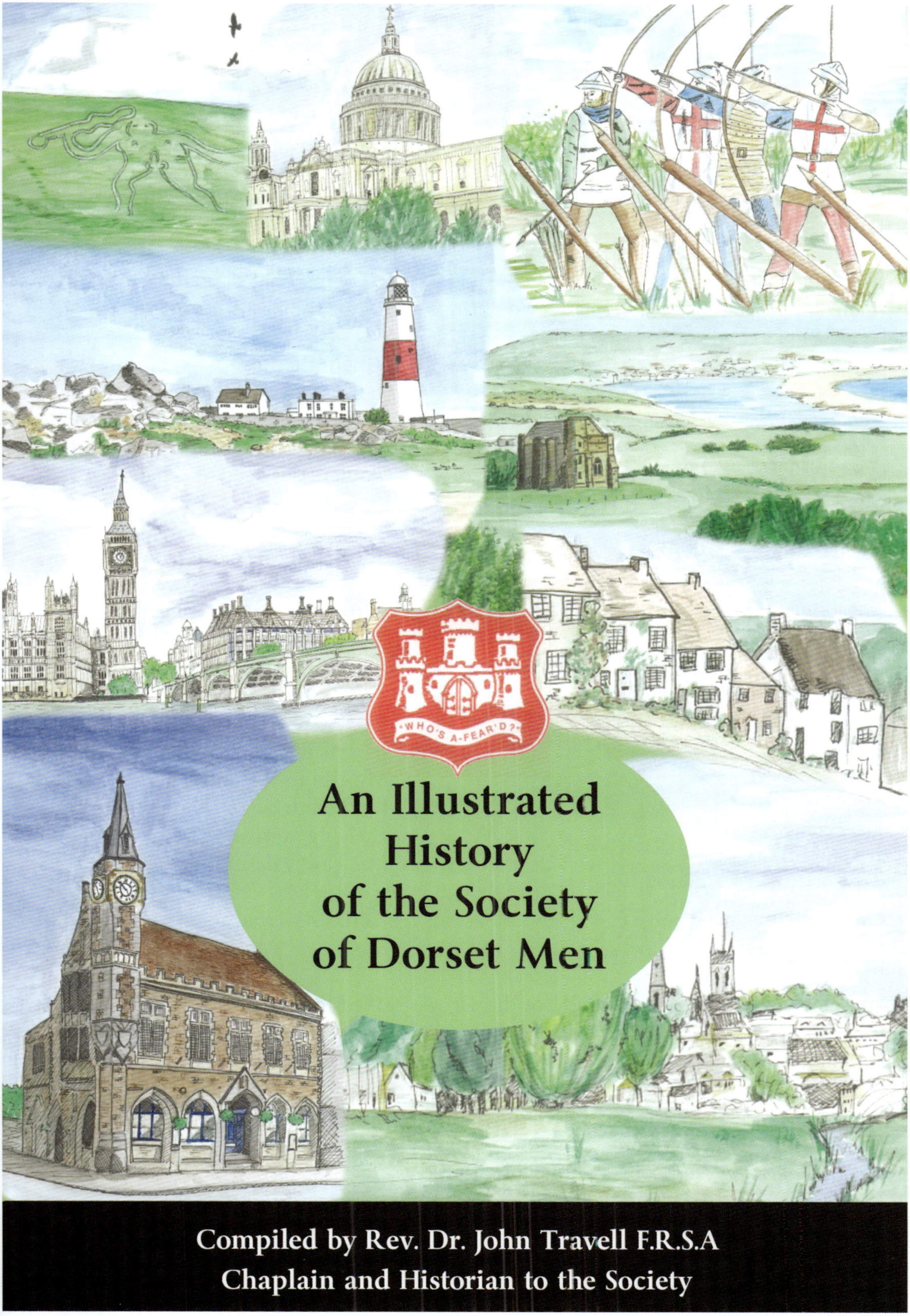
WHO'S A-FEAR'D?
An Illustrated History of the Society of Dorset Men
Compiled by Rev. Dr. John Travell F.R.S.A
Chaplain and Historian to the Society

A Childhood Memory of WW2 in Wool

By Alan Brown

In 1944 I was seven years old and living in East Burton Road at Wool. We lived quite close to Wool railway station so were used to seeing plenty of troops from Bovington and Lulworth camps.

If they were in large numbers waiting for special trains, they would sit on the banks under the hedges between the station and Woolbridge and along the East Burton Road.

Wool Station 1944

When the troops were lining the banks we could earn quite useful pocket money by buying cigarettes for them from local shops and they would let us keep the change.

Then one day the Americans arrived. The first stayed close by for a few days at Woolbridge. They were practising putting a Bailey Bridge across the River Frome just down river from the existing bridge.

They were camped in the field across the road from Woolbridge Manor. My brother, Mike and I would visit them after school hoping for chewing gum and sweets. We rarely came away disappointed.

On one occasion, it must have been a Saturday, a sergeant asked us if we would like something to eat, so of course we said "Yes!"

We sat on the bridge parapet and our dinner was served in mess tins. This was the first time we had seen pineapple and were not quite sure whether to eat it as it was served with ham and cheese potato. It was certainly not the sort of food we were used to, but we thoroughly enjoyed it.

The next day they were gone but a few days later another group arrived and camped on the top end of the Moors by East Burton Road.

They had a large anti-aircraft gun under the trees in the Old Drove just 100 yards from our home so our excitement and sweet supply continued for a few more days. Then suddenly they were also gone.

This must have been just before D=Day and there was a great deal of activity around the station. Our parents made us cross the railway by the stile and over the fields in the Folly to get to school rather than go by the road and across the railway crossing.

Certainly the war was on our doorstep at this time for our headmistress, Miss Bohs, wrote in her Day Book on May 18, 1944. "Tension rather great this week owing to severe raids of late. Two people killed and three injured at East Burton and a house destroyed by a direct hit on Monday morning".

The inhabitants were Mr & Mrs Ricketts and they lived in a railway house beside the crossing over the railway line on Burton Common, a couple of hundred yards west of the Seven Stars.

The railway crossing remains and is now a footpath into Dorset Green Technology Centre, but at the time of the bombing, the heath was a dummy airfield to attract enemy bombers away from Warmwell aerodrome.

There was great concern that night as we could hear the bombs explode nearby. Whether we knew the implications of what was happening I don't remember.

However, one day my father, who worked on the railway at Wool said there was a hospital train at the station so of course we had to go and look. We got out the go-cart (box on pram wheels) with my brother Mike riding and me pushing and headed for the station.

Sure enough, there stood the train in the up-side siding with large red crosses on the sides and by climbing the steps to the signal box we could see red crosses on the roof.

Soon American Army ambulances started to arrive.
The ambulances drove down through the railway yard the whole length of the train and the wounded soldiers were lifted out on stretchers and put on the train.

One of the wounded who sticks in my mind kept kicking his legs in the air as he was tranferred to the train. Most were on stretchers but some were walking and they all had field dressings on their heads or arms in slings.

Strangely enough, although there were half a dozen of us boys hanging around and watching no one told us to clear off or tell us we were in the way.

The wounded had been flown from the beaches of Normandy into Warmwell aerodrome. From Warmwell they were transferred to Moreton House where a field hospital had been set up in the park.

My cousin who lives in Moreton told me that the Americans had laid on water, sewage pipes and electricity into the tents where the wounded were tended before being put back into the ambulances and driven to Wool Station.

At the time, Moreton House was occupied by the 9th Air Corps Military Police and they had taken it over from the RAMC. - (Royal Army Medical Corps).
They were certainly most generous with their rations and the gifts were greatly appreciated by the recipients.

Tinned fruit was very scarce and most people relied on fresh fruit or the fruit they had preserved themselves in Kilner jars.

Suddenly, the Americans were gone.

The hospital was dismantled and the convoys of American ambulances no longer lined the East Burton Road.

I don't remember how long the D-Day activities carried on around Wool Station or how many hospital trains left, but the memory of the activities remain clear to this day.

I never remember being frightened, not even when we were called upon in the middle of the night to go into the air raid shelter.We always carried our gas masks and every week at school we had gas mask and fire drill.

We had a wonderful freedom to wander across the fields and through the woods collecting the silver strips that had been dropped by aircraft for what we thought was to confuse enemy Radar. How true this was we never knew. Once we had collected enough we took it to the local Police Station.

I do remember hiding under a hayrick at Woodstreet when a dogfight was taking place overhead. If we were out in the open fields and the Spitfires were returning low towards Warmwell we would wave our shirts and occasionally a pilot would waggle his wings to us. How we would cheer when this happened. We liked to think it was the same pilot each time. I think life must have seemed very quiet when it was all over.

Staff at Wool Station 1944

Sadly, the large Ash trees under which the anti-aircraft gun was concealed were wantonly and unnecessarily cut down this year (75th Anniversary of D-Day), and with them disappeared the carved initials of some of the American GIs who were there in 1944. A little bit of history gone for ever.

The Thomas Hardy Society

By Faysal Mikdadi

Inspired by Thomas Hardy – Students' Poetry Workshops

In November 2018, The Thomas Hardy Society decided to spread an appreciation of Hardy's works amongst young readers. Faysal Mikdadi, the newly appointed Academic Director, was asked to run school-based Thomas Hardy Poetry Workshops. #

Thomas Hardy with Book

Nine schools agreed to take part in the project. Four were in Dorset: Bryanston, Dorchester Middle School, St Osmund's Church of England Middle School and Thomas Hardye School. The other five were made up of three in Cornwall, one in Taunton and one in Birmingham.

A total of just over one hundred students aged between 10 and 18 took part in the Workshops which resulted in the publication of 134 students' poems.

At the same time, the National Trust put on its first Thomas Hardy Poetry Competition for students aged between 13 and 19 who lived in or attended schools in Dorset.

The Anthology of the students' poems, Inspired by Thomas Hardy, included the six finalists of the National Trust Thomas Hardy Poetry Competition 2019 and one poem by a six-year-old poet who submitted her poem at The Thomas Hardy Victorian Fair of Sunday 2 June 2019.

A typical poetry workshop session would start with engaging the students in a general discussion on reading and writing poetry.

The following were agreed with students as the main aims of each session:

- ✓ Engaging students within a relaxed and friendly ambience.
- ✓ Eliciting from students an acknowledgement of having read and written poems.
- ✓ Getting students to talk about favourite poems read.
- ✓ Encouraging students to discuss their own writing (of verse or prose).
- ✓ Getting students to talk about what inspires them to write.
- ✓ Getting students to talk about a favourite poem.
- ✓ Imbuing students with a sense of worth through their views of poetry and of writing in general being sought, appreciated and respected.

- ✓ Engaging reluctant students.
- ✓ Discussing how poems are composed.
- ✓ Showing that writing poetry is both an art form as well as a formulaic process that could be engaged with through inspiration and without.
- ✓ Sharing a few Thomas Hardy poems as exemplars worthy of emulation.

Each student was given a booklet put together by The Thomas Hardy Society which included the following Thomas Hardy poems:

An August Midnight
The Self-Unseeing
The Orphaned Old Maid
The Fiddler
A Church Romance
When I Set out for Lyonesse
Beeny Cliff
A Poet
At the Railway Station, Upway
On a Discovered Curl of Hair

Students started by having a general conversation about poetry. The idea was to try to find each students' 'inner spark of divine fire' to share and celebrate in order to hear and validate the individual student's voice.

Amongst the principles agreed with each Poetry Workshop group were the following two: (1) There is no good poetry or bad poetry: there is only self-expression within a free and mutually supportive group. (2) Composing a poem can be quite artificial, e.g. occasional poetry on 'demand'. As an example, the group would share Carol Ann Duffy's 'The Wound in Time' on the occasion of the Armistice Day Centenary.

Students read some or all of the poems listed. Reading the poems aloud was a way of giving students confidence in public performances. Whenever a poem was read, the listeners were asked to evaluate first the reading and then the poem itself. They were constantly urged to give reasons for everything that they said rather than simply give out judgements.

The most popular poem amongst the young poets was Hardy's 'An August Midnight'. The following is a replica of what the students had in their booklet:
An August Midnight

I

A shaded lamp and a waving blind,
And the beat of a clock from a distant floor:
On this scene enter - winged, horned, and spined -
A longlegs, a moth, and a dumbledore; dumbeldore: bumblebee
While 'mid my page there idly stands
A sleepy fly, that rubs its hands...

II

Thus meet we five, in this still place,
At this point of time, at this point in space.
- My guests besmear my new-penned line,
Or bang at the lamp and fall supine.
'God's humblest, they!' I muse. Yet why?
They know Earth-secrets that know not I.

besmear: smear over / stain
supine: lazily inactive / listless

Max Gate, 1899

Notes (based on The Poetry of Thomas Hardy – A Handbook and Commentary by J. O. Bailey, The University of North Carolina Press, Chapel Hill, USA, 1970.)

'Hardy's reverence for all life had some basis in his reading in science, in evolutionary theory, all living things are akin…' Hardy once remarked "'I often wonder how much animals know – about things – things of which we are 'ignorant'". The "Earth secrets" that he supposed the insects might know are not earth's meanings. They do not know more than the poet does, but each perceives something the other does not.'

After reading the poem several times, a series of questions were asked under two headings: (1) Facts / Surface Meanings: (a) Where is the poet in this narrative? (In his study.) (b) What is he doing? (Writing.) (c) Who or what comes in? (Four creatures/ insects.) (d) What is the fly doing? (Rubbing its hands.) (d) What happens to the poet's page of writing? (The ink is smudged.) These questions were relatively easy to go through and the students were invariably praised for understanding the 'events' of the poem. (2) Deeper Meanings: (a) What do you think the poet is trying to tell us? (A little observation or vignette of something that happened late at night in his study.) (b) Can you support your response with a quotation from the poem? (He describes the light and sounds in the room and then tells us 'On this scene enter…' (c) What does the poet think that these four creatures are to start with? ('God's humblest, they!') (d) When he changes his mind, what does he think about these creatures? ('They know Earth-secrets that know not I.')

Through discussions and further questioning, students were given opportunities to expand on their understanding of the poem in any way that they wished on condition that whatever they said was supported from the text in front of them.

Working alone or in pairs, the students replaced the first six lines of the poem with their own observation of anything that came to their mind. They could, if they wished, use Hardy's language if they needed to, e.g. they could write, 'An old desk lamp and a dusty blind, / And the sound of mum's TV the other side of my wall: / On this scene enter – fluttering, mewing, and growling / My horrible brother, with his I-Phone and grumpy mood…' The lines did not need to rhyme.

This process was repeated with other poems. As each poem is read, discussed, analysed and 're-written', students were encouraged to take risks and 'improve' on Hardy using their own poetic genius.

Here are a few examples of what the students wrote, inspired by Hardy's "An August Midnight":

After 'An August Midnight'

Serena Forwood (Bryanston School)

A ray of sun and the mutter of leaves
The mark of a minute, faster than it seems
On this scene enter – nerves, anticipation and dread –
Children, pupils, peers; all longing for bed.
Row upon row, behind and beside
Away from sun, trapped inside…
'An August Midnight'

Collaborative Work by St Ives Students

A dirty lamp and tattered blind,
A broken chime from a distant ground,
Patterned, spiked, winged – entered the scene
A bumblebee, a caterpillar and a ladybird.
While within my dark works they shine innocent,
Insignificant, slumped there without sense,
As time slows, I sit in the company of my neighbours,
During the span, as I forget my labours,
One line broken, one sound misheard
Or shelter under the lamp, ambivalent yet assertive
'Lucky are they, in their oblivion' and yet
Our ignorance seems to be set.

The Night of the Insects

Harry Dyer (Trewirgie Junior School)

A bright phone and a blinding light,
With a moth a fly and a longlegs on this Tuesday night,
The humble moth repeatedly ramming in to the lamp,
The fly is crawling on the old Gramp,
The longlegs is just being big,
Whilst the fly is hiding under a wig,
How they're still awake at this late hour,
Is a thing called insect power!!!

Another very popular Hardy poem was 'The Self-Unseeing' which appeared in the Students' Booklet as follows:

The Self-Unseeing

Here is the ancient floor,
Footworn and hollowed and thin,
Here was the former door
Where the dead feet walked in.
She sat here in her chair,
Smiling into the fire;
He who played stood there,
Bowing it higher and higher.

Childlike, I danced in a dream;
Blessings emblazoned that day;
Everything glowed with a gleam;
Yet we were looking away!

emblazoned: displayed brightly

Notes

This poem 'presents Hardy's nostalgic meditation during a visit to his boyhood home at Higher Bockhampton… The characters are himself, his father, and his mother.' Hardy as a child was no more than four years old dancing to his father's playing of the violin.

This poem evoked many memories of recent childhood which students wished to share through their poems. However, the poem also inspired some young poets to write on a different subject whilst emulating Hardy's style, structure and form rather than purely using his meaning. Here are a few examples of what some composed:
Three students from St Osmund's also based their poems on 'The Self-Unseeing': Hedley Richardson, Sophia Thorpe and Freddie Warburton.

When You Said Your Last Goodbye
Hedley Richardson

A singing bird, a waving tree,
A happy time, just you and me.
A howling wind, a crashing sea,
By your side, wherever you may be.

You woke up with a tear drop in your eye,
I woke up next to you wondering why?
I am very worried, rather annoyed,
You stop speaking and start to avoid.

Something is wrong, not quite right,
You move away, we start to fight.
Which path do I follow? I am lost.
I cry an ocean and miss you lots.

When you whispered your last goodbye,
You left and you made me cry.
Being with you is the most treasured time,
I thought that you would always be mine.

There Is Not Much That I Can Do

By Sophia Thorpe

There is not much that I can do
With my ideas, so few
In a world where I am insignificant
All I seem to do is rant.

But still, is there hope?
Or am I just on a downward slope?
Could a person change their fate?
Or is it just too late?

I will make a change,
My words will not derange,
I can make a difference,
I will make the world see sense.

I Know That You Mean Well

Freddie Warburton

I know that you mean well,
Coming up to me with the hounds of hell,
The road to hell has good intentions to sell,
And when it sells it will ring its bells.

It's just you hurting yourself,
You staring back at you in the depths
of hell,
Your mind creating a way to repent,
Going through this eternal torment.

Another one is falling now,
When you see the devil you bow,
Then you will be thrown into a lava pit,
Your own inner demons come with a whip.

You knew what you did was wrong,
It might not have taken too long,
You lived with it for the rest of your life,
And now you suffer eternal strife.

During the Workshops there were occasions when interludes were needed, the process of reading and emulating Hardy's poems was replaced with one of the following two light-hearted verse 'games': (1) Exquisite Corpses: A student would write a first line of a poem. The paper was passed on to a student who wrote a second line. Before he/she passed the paper on to the next, he/she bent the paper so that the first line could not be seen and the next writer saw only the previous line just written. The third writer wrote a line continuing the second line and bent the paper so that his/her line was the only that could be seen by the fourth writer…etc… At the end of the process the paper returned to the one who had written the first line. Who read out the finished poem. A discussion on whether the poem made sense, was cohesive…etc… As a group, the poem might be edited to 'improve' it. (2) Collaborative Genius: A first line was written and the paper was passed on without hiding any previous writing. As the paper went around the room, each student added one line…etc… The paper came back to the first writer who then read it out. A discussion similar to that for (1) above took place.

The following questions were asked before moving on to the next Hardy poem: (1) Do poems have to make sense? (2) Do poems have to rhyme? (3) What matters more; the meaning or the sound? (4) How long or short should a poem be? (5) What possible poetic devices can the students think of – with examples where possible?

The students were given between thirty minutes and one hour to compose their own individual poems. On some rare occasions, two close friends could collaborate on writing a single poem. Students could produce whatever they wished. If they needed a framework or writing scaffold, they might use any Hardy poem from the little booklet, emulate it or, if they felt the need, borrow from it. Students were asked to ensure that what they borrowed was clearly placed within inverted commas to acknowledge that the words were not theirs.

Once the writing session was over, each student was encouraged to read his/her work to the others. After each reading, students were asked to give only positive comments to start with. Whatever comment they made, they had to offer evidence from the text. After all the positive comments are made, students were asked to be critical friends and to suggest what could be done better (always with clear reference to the text being critically appreciated).

Students' word-processed their poems on the day of the Workshop. The poems were included in the Anthology Inspired by Thomas Hardy exactly as they were submitted. Where there appeared to be any apparent errors or omissions, the poet is asked if this were intentional (poetic licence) or if they wished the error or omission rectified.
Where possible and weather permitting students were accompanied out for a walk in search of inspiration. At the Dorchester Middle School, students went out on to the school field. One student explained how she was tasked to count the number of grass blades around the field. She and her friends solved the problem by measuring a very small and manageable area of the field, counting the blades in it, obtaining the overall area of the field from various plans and using the available information to calculate the number of grass blades by carrying out the necessary mathematical operation based on the number of grass blades in the small area multiplied by the overall area…etc… In turn, this discussion led to a group poem:

Blades of Grass

Dorchester Middle Students

Everything stops
When it's cut.
Morning Dew.
Green knees.
Bugs crawling around.

Flowers blooming across the field.
Waving in the breeze.
Dig your hand into the grass.
You forget the number you're on.

Students at the Thomas Hardye School went for a walk trying to work out what inspiration actually was. The walk was led by a student who took everyone towards a green landscape with a few trees. When asked what inspired them about the area, students pointed out two trees standing apart, a clump of trees to the left, a rigidly straight line of young trees to the side, an undulating landscape, the 'fake' exterior of Poundbury houses looking, in the students' words, 'like a clumsy theatre set with their unconvincing classical columns', a group of daffodils standing in rigid formation, the blue sky and wonderful sunshine. A student gave an impromptu recitation of a favourite poem of his 'A Poison Tree' by Blake. Students invariably evaluated the Thomas Hardy Poetry Workshops in positive terms. The following are a few of the participants' evaluations: 'the teacher is funny', 'enjoyable', 'free to express myself', 'analysis of the poems gave me ideas', 'loved the 'no wrong answers' idea', 'the group poem was fun', 'I really enjoyed changing Hardy's old poem', 'my favourite was rewriting the Lyonnesse poem', 'great discussions', 'I enjoyed the critical friend bit', 'Thomas Hardy is a really good poet', 'I like expressing my thoughts', 'the teacher is really enthusiastic', 'pleasant to listen to each other', "The Self-Unseeing' made me want to be a child again but this time I am looking', "The Self-Unseeing' shows that anything can happen in a child's world', 'the teacher's passion for poetry is infectious', 'can we have more lessons like this next year?', 'It is fantastic to be able to re-write the Greats…', 'this was real fun', 'the teacher was a bit crazy whenever he read our poems – really cool', 'I really enjoyed expressing myself'…

The Avenue of Inspiration

Four Dorset pupils - finalists in the National Trust Competition.

As the Anthology Inspired by Thomas Hardy was being compiled and prepared for publication by September 2019, an e-mail was received from a Sixth Former who wrote: 'I just want to take this opportunity to thank you for doing this Workshop. This is the first poetry I have ever written and not only have I enjoyed the process but I feel real accomplishment as a writer. I hope you continue the sessions so others can enjoy the experience too.'

These students are the poets of tomorrow. Their writings will be the inspiration to the next generation of Thomas Hardy Poetry Workshops in decades to come.

(Editorial Note: Dr. Faysal Mikdadi was appointed The Thomas Hardy Society's Academic Director in November 2018. He is a widely published novelist and poet. His works are featured in several poetry anthologies including two devoted entirely to his poems. Amongst his publications are the novels Chateaux en Palestine, Return and Tamra, the poetry anthologies A Return and Painted into a Corner, and the bibliographies Margaret Thatcher and Gamal Abdel Nasser. He is a regular presence at poetry reading around the dining table at Max Gate where the Thomas Hardy Poetry Group meets monthly. He is also a member of the Dorchester Poets Group that meets every third Wednesday of the month and whose first anthology A Perfect Day was recently co-edited by Faysal Mikdadi and Julian Nangle (published 2018). In 2019 Faysal Mikdadi edited Julian Nangle's poetry anthology Poppy and other poems of grief and celebration.)

Rowan House Dorchester and Captain Gerald O'Sullivan VC

By Richard Pilcher

This article outlines the history of Rowan House, in Dorchester, including those who have had their home here with particular reference to Captain Gerald O'Sullivan VC, to date, Dorchester's sole recipient of the Victoria Cross.

Rowan House boutique share-living 2019
(Photo by Trevor Matthews)

Rowan House circa 1905

Jeremy Pope standing with award-winning Dorchester Town Crier, Alistair Chisholm.
(Photo Courtesy Trevor Matthews)

The house stands on land where during the Roman period an earth bank and ditch would run surrounding the then settlement of Durnovaria. The land has also been used for burial of the poor, sited just outside the ancient Dorchester fortifications. Early town maps reveal a settlement on Rowan's existing site, predating construction of the present house.

Rowan House is thought to have been built in the earlier 1870s while still under the ownership of the Prince of Wales Estate, and was designed as a family house. The architect was George John Gregory Gregory.

It lies adjacent to the new Brewery Square development formerly the site of Eldridge Pope brewery which in the early 1870s was also all part of the Duchy of Cornwall Estate. It was sold in two lots: 11 acres in 1874 and a further 20 acres in 1879. The land on both occasions was bought by Alfred Pope and his brother Edwin.

The first parcel of land included the area on which Rowan House lies. The second parcel of land included the proposed site for "a new brewery" which was to open in 1881, adjacent to the newly built railway line to Dorchester at South Station.

This second parcel of land also contained plans for building houses along Prince of Wales Road. Discussion is ongoing whether this included Rowan House. Palace records are reported to indicate it was under the possession of the then Prince of Wales, Prince Edward, at the time of being built and this could well explain why no building application has yet been located in town records, in notable variance to the surrounding development.

In July 1882, Andrews & Pope Solicitors published details of the Prince of Wales Road Victorian expansion showing houses already built along with listings of their respective owners. The owner of Rowan House is recorded as being John George Gregory Gregory. The house is listed as standing on the edge of an area of land of about one acre providing space for a kitchen garden and small orchard.

Gregory was not only a qualified architect; he was also an Alderman, and Mayor of Dorchester, five times between 1872 and 1895.

He was also an important local benefactor. In his last year of office, he paid £3,400 to buy four acres of land off the Duchy of Cornwall for the corporation for their use as pleasure gardens. These were opened in 1896. A fountain was built there in his memory by his friend Charles Hansford

On Gregory's death, the estate passed to his widow Eliza Gregory. She in turn sold the house before she died in January 1901, to a Miss Margaret Jane Ashley, who was at the time living in nearby Stratton, Dorset.

The Gregory Memorial Fountain circa 1905

During her twelve years ownership Miss Ashley made many changes to the house including adding domestic offices which are known today as the Lodge, new up-to-date "sanitary fittings and "top of the range" kitchen fittings. She built a brick and tiled stable block consisting of two stalls and a loose box in part of the kitchen garden now occupied by Age UK. She also built a detached cottage in the grounds for her groom/gardener, which we know now as Rowan Cottage and annex. In the 1911 census, the house is listed as having 17 rooms with four living-in staff.

In May 1913, the executors of Miss Ashley's Estate sold the house at auction. The particulars of the sale listed the house as consisting of on the ground floor a dining room, a double sitting room, fuel store, and a strong room. In the basement wine and beer cellars. On the first floor there were three bedrooms, a boudoir dressing room and bathroom. On the second floor, there were five bedrooms for servants. At the same time, the extensive contents were sold by Messrs Dukes.

Miss Ashley was responsible for building three Almshouses in Stratton on the site of The Smith's Arms. In 1920, a charity was set up in her memory to administer them. A century later "The Margaret Jane Ashley Almshouse Charity" continues to provide this facility.

The house was then bought in 1913 by Mrs Charlotte Johanna O'Sullivan, widow of the late Lieutenant Colonel George Lidwill O'Sullivan of the 1st Argyll Highlanders who had died in 1901.

Mrs O'Sullivan had seven children. Gerald Robert O'Sullivan (1888-1915) was the youngest of her two sons. "Gerry" was educated at Wimbledon College and at Sandhurst Royal Military Academy: "his parents aspired a military career".

In May 1909, he was gazetted to the 1st Battalion Royal Inniskilling Fusiliers and posted to Tienstin, North China in September. He served there during the Chinese rebellion until 1912 followed by a posting to Secunderabad, Central India, until 1914. He then returned with his regiment to Rugby England from where he spent time on leave visiting his mother and family at Rowan House.

He departed for the Gallipoli Campaign with his regiment on St Patrick's Day, 17th March 1915, forming part of "the incomparable 29th Division". They landed at X Beach Cape Helles on 25th April.

He was awarded the Victoria Cross on 1st /2nd July. This can be viewed at the Lord Ashcroft Gallery at the Imperial War Museum along with the following accolade:

"On July 1st/2nd 1915 at Krithria he volunteered to lead a party at night to retake a vital trench, armed with only jam-tin bombs. At one point he stood up out of the trench to throw his bombs more accurately. He was wounded but kept going to take the trench .

On the 21st August the 29th Division was tasked with taking Scimitar Hill (Hill 70) which involved landing at Suvla Bay and advancing inland across the dried-up Salt Lake to approach Hill 70. The 5th Dorsetshire Regiment and later the Queens Own Dorsetshire Yeomanry also took part in the attack.

British forces at Sulva Bay on 21st August 1915 *(photograph courtesy of the Keep Military Museum of Devon and Dorset Dorchester)*

Following the attack Captain O'Sullivan was reported missing. Conflicting accounts for some time gave rise to the hope he was a prisoner in the hands of the Turkish troops. His body was never found. His mother's anguish would be tempered, like many mothers throughout Europe and beyond at the time, with a lingering hope of seeing her son return home.

Jam-tin bombs illustrated here were "emergency" grenades used on the front line at Gallipoli using discarded food containers.

This map demonstrates how the surrounding hills provided an "ampitheatre view of the attacking British with the defending Turkish forces all in the best seats".

Lord Ashcroft collection at the Imperial War Museum. *Photo obtained by Antoinette, with kind permission from Museum Curator, in support of research behind Blue Plaque.*

Captain O'Sullivan VC displayed on town Cenotaph overlooked by The Rowan House where the posthumous VC was received by mother.
(Photo by Antoinette)

On 1st September 1915, his award of the Victoria Cross was published in the London Gazette and on the 26th September 1916 it was delivered by registered post to "The Rowan House".

Although there is no known grave, Captain O'Sullivan is remembered on the War Memorial to the missing at St Helles in Gallipoli, the National Arboretum in Staffordshire, and in the church at the Royal Military Academy Sandhurst. There is a plaque in his honour in the Roman Catholic church in Sherborne. His name can also be found on the War Memorial opposite Rowan House.

Mrs O'Sullivan was of South African descent. She would have had knowledge of both the then recent Boer War and also details of the planning and execution of the Gallipoli campaign both from a military and political viewpoint. Her thoughts are not recorded.

In April 1919, Rowan House was sold to Robert Gale Cave, a retired farmer from Almer near Sturminster Newton. Before he died in 1926, he bequeathed the house to his wife Amy Rachel Cave who in turn in March 1949, left the house to a niece, Ethel Mary Lewis.

Her niece was a qualified nurse. She saw the need for nurses' accommodation for those working at the Dorset County Hospital and in November 1949 sold the house to provide bedsits for hospital staff.

Ownership over the next 64 years passed through five NHS Trusts. During the late 80s proposals were afoot to demolish Rowan to install a large traffic roundabout at the junction of the five roads. In 1996, West Dorset District Council Environmental Health Department inspected Rowan House and this resulted in various alterations and improvements to provide further multiple living units through division of major rooms, supported by three shared kitchens and bathrooms. The property subsequently succumbed to a lack of maintenance, and when no longer required for nurses' accommodation, and suffering considerable water ingress through both roof and chimneys, the County Hospital decided to dispose of the building on the open market. Rowan was once again under threat from possible demolition and redevelopment.

Such fate was avoided when John Cobley and his fiancée, Annette Weller, assumed ownership of Rowan House in 2014. They set out to restore the house to its former glory re-instating many of its original Victorian features. False partitioning in major rooms was removed, and period features such as plaster cornicing and slate fireplaces, reinstated. Victorian postcards were used to guide external restoration work, including relaying of original ornate-tiled roof and reconstruction of an earlier demolished rear veranda/orangery.

15 en-suite bedrooms with breakfast bar facilities were installed, supported by four modern communal kitchens in each main area, and onsite parking. Security is achieved through incorporating Security Key systems throughout, and fire safety assured through installation of a sophisticated alarm-detection systems and water sprinklers. Amenity is enhanced through provision of fibre optic data connections to each room. The house now delivers a significant contribution to the town council's stated priority for provision of affordable town centre accommodation, to support the young labour force essential for the operation of commerce within Dorchester today.

In the course of extensive restoration work, a particular feature of interest was discovered on the top floor. On removing a partition composed of elm lather and plaster, a void was discovered. Within it appeared a small poorly rough-sawn table laid in a manner suggestive of a single setting. The lathes used for the enclosing partition suggest insertion before World War II. The significance of these findings remains unclear. One suggestion links this small discovery to Mrs O'Sullivan's obvious grief, and possible inner hopes that should her lost son's presence ever return to the family home, there would remain timeless access to hospitality, even extending beyond her own

HRH Duke of Gloucester meets Major Keith Wilson (Retired) of the Society of Dorset Men, who inspired and delivered the Blue Plaque. Standard Bearers were organised and led by Tony Seal, Area Ceremonial Officer. *(Photo courtesy Steve Lee)*

Canon Tom Woodhouse, HRH Duke of Gloucester, and Annette at the Blue Plaque unveiling (Photo courtesy Steve Lee)

departure.

On 30th May 2019, a Blue Plaque was unveiled in his honour at Rowan House by HRH the Duke of Gloucester. Attendance at the ceremony included members of the 1st Irish Inniskilling Fusiliers Association.

Rowan House can be seen today standing proudly between the two main shopping areas of Dorchester bridging Trinity Street and the new Brewery Square development. Examination of the War Memorial opposite, the Borough Gardens and the Blue Plaque, provide reminders of some of its rich history. The future can be seen in its newly restored structural condition and those members of the young working community of Dorchester who currently enjoy living

HRH Duke of Gloucester conveys appreciation to the Durnovaria Silver Band. *(Photo courtesy Steve Lee)*

HRH Duke of Gloucester alongside the Mayor, meeting with invited guests. *(Photo courtesy Trevor Matthews)*

Sea Foal

by Judi Moore

I often walk along the Esplanade at night. I enjoy the sparkling necklace of lights around Weymouth Bay, and the way the streetlights on Portland dither in the constant wind. Out on the island's harbour arms lonely little warning lights wink on and off, red and white. All is peace.

This one evening in early April the most tremendous gale had just blown itself out after rattling the windows for 36 hours. The tide was high and on the turn. The moon was full but small and far away, casting long, pale shadows. Little foam-edged waves washed to and fro in the shallows.

Further out I could hear splashing. Probably a Bay-swimmer or paddle-boarder returning late, I thought. But then I could hear something else. It was loud, the sort of noise that if heard in a dark house you'd think the house was haunted and you'd leave in haste.

The keening continued. It sounded quite desperate to my ears. Perhaps something was in trouble down by the water, or in it? I hurried down the last few yards of the footpath, onto the beach, and tried to work out where the noise was coming from.

I pulled out my mobile phone and switched it on as I stumbled across the shingle. I'd have light in a minute, when it'd booted up. That should help. I stopped and listened. The phone chirped that it was ready, and I fumbled the flashlight on, shining it up and down the beach and in the shallows.

There?

Right up against the groyne, near the high water mark, was a tangle of something which seemed to be moving. Could this be it?

The tangle was netting and buoys, snagged on the rocks. It must have been lost from a fishing boat in the gale. In the middle of the muddle a big dark eye looked up at me. I caught my breath – it was so unexpected, that eye. The awful moaning stopped.

I took a step back and played the flashlight over the tangle of net and rope to try and work out what I was looking at. Where was the body to go with the eye? Deep within the tangle it was writhing desperately; was this its body or legs or … a tail? … I couldn't see.

I had another look at the head of whatever-it-was. It winced when I shone the light in its eye. I apologised softly for blinding and frightening it. I saw it had a long snout. For a second I thought it was a dog. But then I realised whatever-it-was had no ears.

The creature gaped and gave that dreadful cry of distress again. The mouth was full of needle-sharp teeth. I was pretty sure it was something from the sea. An air breather? A seal? Did they have teeth like that? Or perhaps it was an eel? If it was an eel I needed to get it back into the sea as quickly as possible.

I sat down beside it and rummaged in my shoulder bag for the Swiss army knife I always carry. I chose the saw blade and started cutting. The creature was still now, watching me with its big dark eye.

When I'd freed a few of the more painful-looking strands of net, a flipper slithered out of the mare's nest. A seal then. Or a seal pup perhaps. It was still difficult to tell what size the animal inside the ball of net was. I kept on sawing at the harsh nylon strands. I managed to free its tail; at once the creature started writhing like an eel. And it started making that desperate noise again.

I stopped what I was doing and gingerly laid a hand on the little head. It was warm – too warm, I feared. There was no fur there. It felt more like … a slow-worm, perhaps. Sort of dry and slightly scaly. It didn't shake my hand off or try to bite me. It stopped writhing, but the keening continued. I started talking to it.

'Just lie still for a moment,' I said soothingly. 'Then I can cut you free without hurting you. The more you wriggle the worse tangle you get into. Hush now. Hush.'It seemed to calm down. I got on with cutting the tough nylon as quickly as I could. I cut myself several times, but I don't believe I cut the little ……….

Suddenly I knew what it was!

The chap who takes people out on The Fleet in his glass-bottomed boat had spoken of it, and had pointed out a sculpture of it outside the Ferrybridge Inn. The sculpture, about five feet tall, is of a mythical sea beast, the Veasta, which supposedly lives in the Fleet.

I'd thought it a tall tale for tourists – and certainly the sculpture, of an upright creature very like a seahorse, was of something that couldn't possibly exist in the Fleet. It wouldn't have sufficiently powerful fins to swim against the strong currents that wash in and out from Portland Harbour. And the Fleet is far too shallow for any vertical swimmer of that size to be viable. What I was looking at had a head that was definitely horse-like and, now that I could see more of it, a sinuous body ending in a powerful tail. It was definitely a horizontal swimmer.

I was looking at something out of legend.

It must've been swept out of the Fleet in the gale, fallen foul of this tangle of fishing gear and been unable to return to its home with the tide. It fixed me with its big, dark eye and gave a little whimper. It looked exhausted. I began to be afraid it would die before I could free it and redoubled my efforts. Soon my left hand was a mass of cuts and my right was cramped with sawing endless strands of tough nylon. But finally I could see pretty much the whole animal.

It was about the size of a collie dog. It had a pair of powerful front flippers much like a seal, and a muscular tail which still looked more like an eel than anything else. The neck was long, as was the head: the whole creature was a streamlined marvel. And obviously a strong swimmer.

Delicately, I picked it out from the remains of its cocoon. It lay limp in my arms. I carried it down to the sea and laid it at the edge. I didn't want to put it in the sea in case it was so far gone it drowned. Its body rocked back and forth in the shallows as the wavelets broke around it, but it made no movements of its own.

Suddenly, from a few yards out in the Bay, another Veasta rose out of the water – a bigger one – and began humping itself through the shallows towards me on its flippers and tail like a seal. It hissed as it came. It was coming to help its baby.

The little one began to make a weak version of the alarming noise that first alerted me that something was wrong on the beach. The mother – for surely it was she – began to make crooning noises.

Mother Veasta, standing up on her flippers as she was now, was as tall as me. I remembered the array of teeth in the baby's mouth and retreated up the beach a little way. Her teeth would be much bigger and she had no reason to think kindly of me. Mama hauled herself right out of the sea and began to nudge the little one, rolling it gently into deeper water. I was sure it was dying. But when a wavelet broke over it, it seemed to revive a little. She continued to push it gently out into the Bay.

At that point there was a great commotion off the end of the groyne. A third Veasta reared up out of the water and flopped back down with an almighty crash, like a whale breaching. Presumably this was how the family's guardian male let predators know to leave them alone. I shuffled further back up the beach, picking up my phone and knife as I went and stuffing them into my (now soaked) shoulder bag.

It was quite difficult, backing up the beach while keeping an eye on the family of Veastas, stallion, mare and foal. The stallion breached several more times and, finally charged the beach. I stumbled through the shingle away from him and up onto the footpath. The mare continued to coax the foal into deeper water, keeping it afloat on her neck when it flagged.I watched from the footpath above the beach until the little family had swum completely out of sight.

Painting by Emily King

It wasn't until I got home that I realised I hadn't taken a photograph of the amazing things I'd seen. That's why I'm writing it all down for you now. But I don't suppose for a moment that you'll believe me!.

Two Ladies of Moreton

By Brian Bates

The village of Moreton is best known as the burial place of Thomas Edward Lawrence, popularly known as Lawrence of Arabia. Standing by his impressive grave one can ponder on his adventures in the Great War, which made him internationally famous.

Not ten yards from Lawrence's grave is another headstone, not nearly as prominent, a small, open book with a simple inscription. The name on it belongs to Annie Elizabeth Keats and it too has a story to tell about the Great War and how it brought together two women of very different social classes.

According to the 1911 census the eighteen-year-old Annie Keats was residing in Wheelbarrow Lane, (now re-named The Street), Moreton. Living with her in the five roomed thatched agricultural labourer's cottage were her father James, who worked as a labourer on the Frampton Estate, her mother Rosina and her brother Sidney. As a child, when it came to schooling, she and her brother did not have to walk very far as the village schoolhouse was just around the corner. The building is now used as a tea rooms but the inside betrays its former use as a school, not just by its architecture but also by the old school photographs displayed on the walls, one of which includes Annie and Sidney.

Next to the former village school, behind a high wall, hides the spacious rectory of the local church of St Nicholas where twenty-nine-year-old Winifrede Marsden lived with her family. The census shows that the Marsdens were of a very different social class to the Keats family. The Rectory had 13 rooms and the head of household was Horace Marsden In addition to Horace and Winifrede were Horace's wife Frances, his other daughter Evelyn and four servants.

In such a small village there is no doubt that the two women knew one another but their world's were clearly defined by their respective positions in society. Despite this, one catastrophic event was to bring the two women together, and that was the Great War.

Ten years before that terrible conflict took place, and following the South African wars, the government realised that the existing civilian medical services could not cope with large numbers of casualties in the event of a major conflict. Accordingly, through the Red Cross, Voluntary Aid Detachment services were established, which would be mobilised when needed. These included nursing and ambulance services, and the creation of hospitals scattered throughout the country, and when WW1 started in August 1914 the VAD services swung into action. In the case of hospitals, many of these consisted of large houses vacated by their owners and handed over to the authorities. One such owner was Denzil Hughes-Onslow who lived with his wife Marion at Colliton House, in Dorchester. Denzil was a well-known and popular Durnovarian who invested a lot of time and money in the town, particularly in sport, and when hostilities were declared he and Marion had no hesitation in handing over their property to the Red Cross to be used as a hospital.

Colliton VAD Hospital number 92 opened its doors on 7 November, 1914 with 20 beds and its Commandant was Winifrede Marsden, in charge of everything except the medical and nursing services. These were run by the doctor in charge, Dr William Borough-Cousins and a Matron. Among Winifrede's duties was that of recruiting new staff and it was not long before she persuaded Annie to join her at Colliton as a VAD nurse. Annie started just a week after her boss, doing ward work, at a salary of £18 per annum. Before being accepted into the service she first had to face an interviewing panel, doubtless headed by Winifrede, and was required to provide two references. She then to pay 1 shilling and sixpence for her training in first aid and home nursing. VAD nurses tended to come from middle class and upper class families so Winifrede must have thought very highly of the carter's daughter, and one wonders how the young girl from Moreton felt working alongside the likes of Florence Bankes of Welfeton Manor.

Nurse Annie Keats

It appears that at some stage Annie considered offering her services in France or Belgium. The Evidence for this comes from an embroidered postcard she received from her sweetheart Bertie, who was serving in the Royal Garrison Artillery. He wrote:

"My darling, I received your welcome letter last night with which I was very pleased. I am sorry I cannot write a letter in return as I do not feel up to it, so I hope you will like this card. We have been shelled all day long, they have only just given over a few minutes ago. Now, you will be much better off if you stay where you are. It is bad enough there and I'm sure you could not stand it out here, especially now that the cold weather will soon be here. That is the testing time for them all. This is all I can tell you this time, so must draw to a close. With love & kisses – Bert."

It was not long before the first patients were arriving at Dorchester South railway station from the battle fields of France and Belgium. Some of the earliest casualties were Belgian soldiers, although throughout the life of the hospital it was mainly British and Commonwealth troops who were cared for. It was not long before the beds at Colliton were full and it was therefore decided to increase capacity. The answer was to erect marquee tents in the extensive grounds of Colliton Park, which would enable up to 200 patients to be looked after.

Colliton House

One of the largest contingents to arrive in Dorchester numbered 150, in the early summer of 1917, after the Battle of Messines Ridge. One can imagine the sense of nervous excitement felt by Winifrede, Annie and the other nurses when news came that a new batch of patients were on their way. Fortunately, we can get some sense of it from a poem written By Ella Fricker, one of the nurses:

NIGHT CONVOY

Black was the sky, and black the trees,
blackest the ghostful street,
Where echos idly waited for the fall of
passing feet.
Blackness, except where Colliton threw
out a cheerful light,
And nurses by the gateway carried
lanterns twinkling bright.
Waiting and list'ning till at last the eerie
silence broke,
And growing sounds of wheels and steps
the sleeping echoes woke.

Then, rumbling through the narrow
street, the ambulances came,
Monstrous and sinister they looked by
that small flickering flame.
The lads who singing marched away, full
of the joy of life,
Now silent, helpless, anguished, maimed,
have come back from the strife.
Dimly the lanterns lighted up the caverns
where they lay,
While Red Cross Bearers gently-strong
bore one by one away.
Each stretcher by a lantern-bearing
VAD, was led,
And weirdly danced the lights upon still
form and bandaged head.

Another, and another came, loud
trampling through the night,
T'll all the Avenue was starred with
moving points of light.
And wide-spread branches seemed to dip,
saluting as they passed,
To where the lights of Colliton, showed
rest was near at last.
Old home of many memories! – the
proudest and the best,
Will be that priceless, piteous chain that
glittered on your breast.

(Courtesy of Dorset History Centre)

Soldiers with all kinds of injuries and illnesses arrived at Colliton but, generally speaking, VAD hospitals were places where men recuperated. That is not to say that Annie and Winifrede did not witness some terrible injuries and deaths. For example, on 12 July, 1917 the Western Gazette reported that, "A death occurred among the military patients at Colliton VAD Hospital on Monday, when Private Albert Cockell, Worcester Regiment, passed away from complications arising from wounds received while fighting at the Front." Albert was 20 years of age and his body was returned to his parents home in Westbury, Somerset." Unfortunately, not all relatives could afford to pay to have their loved one's bodies returned and their graves are to be found in St George's church cemetery, Fordington.

When they were fit enough the patients were allowed to go into Dorchester, easily identifiable by their blue uniforms. One thing that was forbidden was the consumption of alcohol, so pubs like The Old Ship, a favourite of the military, were strictly out of bounds, a rule which some decided did not apply to them. In Nov, 1917 a Mrs Harriet Collins, licensee of the Dorchester Arms, in North Square, appeared before he Police Court for selling alcohol to wounded soldiers. At the hearing Dr Burrough-Cousins reported that there had already been trouble with patients returning from town much the worse for wear. Another woman, a Mrs Townsend, was charged with harbouring a patient who had gone absent without leave. Despite her denial and floods of tears in the court she was found guilty and fined £5, the equivalent of about £175 today.
Although fraternisation between the nurses and patients was not allowed under VAD rules many a soldiers heart was set a flutter my his nurse. Several of the patients expressed their admiration for Annie and put pen to paper in verse. One love struck man was John McCann of the 2nd Seaforth Highlanders, who wrote:

To Annie.

The sky is high,
The sea is deep.
In your dreams of love to sleep.
If you love me like I love you,
Nothing but death will part us two.

Others were content to express their thanks. Pte. E. Brown of the 9th Suffolk Rgt wrote:

When on my bed of pain I lie
Between the snow white sheets,
Who is it comes to cheer me up,
It is my good nurse Keats.
She smooths the pillars 'neath my sheets
And brings me food to eat,
And if I shiver with a cold
Hot bottles for my feet.
She always wears a smile so sweet,
It makes you glad you're born.
That's why we greet her when she comes,
All hail, oh smiling morn.

(Courtesy of Dorset History Centre)

As important as the men's physical care was their mental welfare and much time was spent by the nursing staff keeping the men occupied. In the summer, of course, they could relax in the grounds of Colliton Park, or perhaps listen to a concert in the Borough Gardens, but in the winter it was more difficult. Card games were always popular and many a whist drive was organised. Annie recorded in an autograph book one such event which occurred just before Christmas, in 1917. The names of the patients and staff who took part are listed, 42 in all, including Annie and Winifrede. Miss Keats was obviously a dab hand at the game and collected first prize. Christmas 1917 was celebrated in some style. The Western Gazette informed its readers that on Christmas Day Winifrede Marsden took presents round to 100 patients after breakfast, personally giving a pair of woollen gloves and a khaki scarf to each. Annie and her colleagues handed out cigarette cases and the ingenious mechanical lighters which were so useful at a time of scarcity of matches. Naturally, the surgeons did the carving at dinner time and plum pudding and ginger wine were in abundance. In the evening Miss Buglar and the Gypsy Concert Party provided the entertainment. On Boxing Day there was another whist drive.

This was not the end of the celebrations, because at New Year Alfred Pope and his wife gave a tea party for 124 patients, an event not missed by the reporters of the County Chronical. It reported that, "a substantial meat tea consisting of turkey and ham was followed by sweets of all kinds.

The pulling of crackers after tea caused great amusement. The patients were waited on by Miss Marsden and her staff, and they thoroughly enjoyed the good things provided. Mr and Mrs Alfred Pope were present at the tea, and they were thanked for their kindness by Canon Hankey and Quarter Master Sergeant Chaplin on behalf of the patients. Afterwards a concert party was given by the Frampton Family Band."

The Popes were not the only Durnovarians to support the hospital. Dorchester folk were ever willing to take the military to their hearts and the men in Colliton were no exception, All kinds of events were held to raise money for their comfort. In October, 1917 a flag day was held in the town in which the patients took part. Also, a number of concerts were held in the Corn Exchange and in August, 1918 a fete was held where one of the attractions was the sale of glass bead chains made by the patients. One national initiative from which the hospital benefitted was the National Egg Collection. Headed by Queen Alexandra the objective was to raise one million eggs a week to send to military patients at home and abroad.

Staff and patients dress up.

Like the German prisoner of war camp in Dorchester the hospital provided a good source of income for local traders during the Great War. Among them were local photographers who visited the Colliton and took photos of the patients often with the nurses. Most of these were straight forward groups but sometimes an element of humour crept in. One shows a group of patients dressed in nurses uniforms, whilst another shows a group of nurses dressed as soldiers and vice versa.

After the armistice was signed Colliton continued nursing wounded soldiers until 30th April, 1919, when it closed and awaited the return of its owners the Hughes-Onslows. But, they never returned. Denzil had been killed on 7 July, 1916, whilst serving with the Dorset Regiment and as a consequence his wife left the town. But, Winifrede Marsden's association with the house did not end there because shortly after the war her father bought the house. By all accounts Winifrede's return to Moreton was quite an event. The village turned out in numbers, lining each side of the street and the local children sang to her. She was also presented with a bouquet of flowers. National recognition for her good work came in the form of an OBE. Winifrede remained in Dorchester where she made a name for herself in local politics and in 1936 she became Dorchester's first lady mayor. She died on 17 August, 1951.

Annie Keats worked at the hospital for a total of 194 weeks and in recognition she was awarded the Red Cross Cross, having already been mentioned in despatches, in October 1917. She must have had some feelings of sadness and anti-climax when she returned to Moreton after the excitement and responsibilities involved in being a nurse. In fact, she carried on nursing, this time for the Frampton family at Moreton House, at least up until the end of the Second World War. Annie never married, it is thought Bert died during the war, and she spent the rest of her life in the village, except for a period during the Second World War when she went to live with her employers in Bournemouth, when Moreton House was taken over by the military. Annie died on 8 June, 1971, aged 78.

For four years Annie Keats and Winifred Marsden had been away from village life, thrust into a huge national initiative to care for men wounded in a terrible conflict. Something that changed their lives forever and something they would never forget. But, just in case they did forget, there was a final poem by Ella Dicker to remind them:

Colliton Hospital

Have you forgotten Colliton, old
Colliton, dear Colliton?
And all it did for England when the
world was wrapped in flame?
Not only doors but human hearts it
open'd to the stricken men,
With tend'rest skill restoring what
the foe had tried to maim.

Work hard! Why yes, of course we
did, but that was just the best of it,
Then everyone was working hard, no
idle hands were seen;
But what delightful fun we had,
when there was time to rest a bit,
And oh! What appetites we had for
bread and margarine.
But we have lost our uniforms, and
Colliton dear Colliton
No longer smells of Chloroform, no
'pictures' there are seen!
No convoy now brings in a load that
breaks one's hearts to look upon;
And where our big white tent-town stood,
the grass is thick and green.

But still my heart holds Colliton, old
Colliton, THE Colliton,
With all its busy Staff at work among the
Lads in Blue,
And ah! that I were back again, with neat
white cap and apron on,
To laugh and work among them all just as
I used to do!

(Courtesy of the Dorset History Centre)

Two distinguished ladies from the village of Moreton…..

General Garibaldi Pays a Brief Visit to Victorian Dorset

by Jack Sweet

The name Garibaldi probably means little to the average Briton in 2020 apart from the name of a biscuit studded with currants or, occasionally, the name of a local pub. In 1864 however, this was a name which rang across Europe; General Giuseppe Garibaldi was hailed as a hero, a general who always won his battles, a freedom fighter, a man who had fought for and secured virtually single-handedly the unification of Italy. The cause for unification in 19th century Europe was an ideal as potent as the search for freedom in Eastern Europe in the days of the Cold War. Garibaldi's words "Liberty does not fail those who are determined to have it", and his famous red shirt inspired a generation.

The General had a remarkable gift of being able to persuade foreign powers that Italian unification was a cause worth fighting for, and without such support it is unlikely that Italy could have achieved unity at that time.

Garibaldi visited England in the spring of 1864. He received a tremendous welcome where ever he went. He was hailed as "one of the world's most popular men", and "one who will live as the incarnate symbol of two passions not likely to die out - the love of country and the love of liberty".

On Monday 25 April the General travelled to Dorset to visit the Channel Fleet at its anchorage off Portland. It was to be a short visit as the great man only wished to see the Royal Navy's new powerful ironclad warships.

The news of the special train conveying him from Bath to Weymouth sped along the line to the stations en route. At Taunton the civic fathers quickly prepared a luncheon in his honour, the church bells pealed and guns fired. A large crowd of dignitaries and townspeople waited eagerly at the railway station for the hero's arrival. Alas, the General never had the pleasure of a Taunton lunch, and never heard the peals of bells because the train stopped short of the town and was redirected onto the Yeovil branch line at Durston which took it on to Weymouth via Pen Mill Station.

Following some confusion regarding the timing of arrival, the train finally steamed into Weymouth Station at half-past five in the late afternoon accompanied by the crash of fog detonators laid on the track, and the roar of the crowd waiting to greet their hero.

Garibaldi and his entourage of friends and supporters, which included his son Ricciotti, the Duke of Sutherland, and somewhat mystifyingly to the Sherborne Mercury, a metropolitan policeman, were welcomed by Flag-Lieutenant Churcher, representing Vice-Admiral Sir Sydney Dacres, CinC Channel Fleet, and were driven to the Quay through the gaily decorated streets and cheering crowds, many of whom were wearing the red shirt in honour of the 'illustrious liberator'.

At the Quay the party embarked on the Admiral's barge and were conveyed the short distance to the gunboat HMS Trincula where Garibaldi was welcomed with a hearty handshake by the commanding officer, Lieutenant Creagh. The Trincula steamed slowly out of the harbour to the cheering of hundreds of spectators lining the Pile Pier, and was followed by the steam yacht Princess carrying more well-wishers.

The Channel Fleet included five powerful ironclad warships - Her Majesty's Ships, Edgar, Black Prince, Defence, Hector and Warrior, the latter being the first of the ironclads and the pride of Queen Victoria's fleet. These were anchored in Portland Roads and as the Trincula cruised past the line strains of the 'Garibaldi Hymn' could be heard coming from the bands of the Edgar and Warrior.

The General was received on board Warrior by Admiral Dacres and was taken to his cabin where he was introduced to members of the Admiral's family before sitting down to a "splendid late luncheon". Following a tour of inspection of the ironclad, the crew beat to quarters and went through the evolutions of a sham fight, firing blank cartridges. Garibaldi was most impressed, remarking that the Warrior was a beautiful ship and the firing was excellent. He was equally impressed by the bearing of the sailors and "considered them the finest in the world".

Upon completion of his inspection Garibaldi bade farewell to the Admiral, "expressing the obligation he was under for the kindness shown towards him", returned to the Trincula and sailed back through a "most delightful evening", arriving at Weymouth Quay at about a quarter to eight.

During the drive to the railway station the General was again cheered all the way. Moreover, it was reported by the Sherborne Mercury, that before his train could pull out well-wishers "clambered up the sides of the carriage, thrusting their hands through the window endeavouring to shake hands with him, whilst the cheering continued and was very great". The train finally got under way bound for Cornwall and the home of his old friend Colonel John Peard at Penquite Manor, where the General would spend a little time before travelling to Plymouth and embarking for home on the Duke of Sutherland's yacht.

Colonel John Peard (1811-1880) was a British soldier who fought alongside Garibaldi in several campaigns and was known as "Garibaldi's Englishman".

William Benn – A Leader of Dissent in 17th Century Dorchester

By David Cuckson

A window in the United Church Dorchester, a building in South Street that was originally Dorchester Congregational Church, commemorates the Reverend William Benn, regarded as the first minister of a separate Congregational Church in Dorchester.

Benn arrived in Dorchester in 1629 to be Rector of All Saints Church in High East Street. A church building still stands on the site, albeit a rebuilding and now disused as a church. He retained his connection with Dorchester until his death in 1681. Immediately prior to his move he had been chaplain to Helena, Marchioness of Northampton, a former Maid of Honour to Elizabeth I but now living in secluded retirement with her family at Redlynch in Somerset: she was an interesting character in that she was born into Swedish nobility and came to England as a young woman where she found herself favoured at court by the Queen. Benn would have been appointed for his credentials as a sound Puritan preacher rather than his social standing. He was born in Egremont, Cumbria in 1600 and was educated at the free school at St Bees before proceeding to attend Queen's College, Oxford as a servitor, a student performing duties for a social superior in exchange for assistance from college funds, and he left Oxford without a degree (although his portrait credits him with an MA).

Rev. John White

Benn's background clearly appealed to the town worthies in Dorchester when they were looking for a new rector for All Saints. David Underdown in his book, Revel, Riot and Rebellion – Popular Politics and Culture in England 1603-1660, says that 'By the 1620s Dorchester was in the grip of an authoritarian Puritan regime which regulated the most minute details of its residents' lives with fanatical rigour.... Of all the towns in the western counties, Dorchester was the one in which Puritan reformation was most systematically imposed.' This was largely due to the leadership and inspiration of the Reverend John White, who was rector of the two other parishes that made up the town of Dorchester, namely St Peter's and Holy Trinity. White would have favoured the appointment of a minister to the remainder of the town who was in sympathy with his reformist path.

In order to understand the character of the town of Dorchester at this time, we need to take into account its earlier history. When John White first arrived in Dorchester it was no different from any other market town of its size, and he encountered opposition from some of the leading burgesses, who objected to their private lives being questioned, and apathy from many of the other citizens who paid little heed to his calls for renewal. There was a lot of poverty and unemployment in the town, and disorder and drunkenness were frequently a source of trouble. But everything changed dramatically with the great fire which swept through the town in 1613, destroying many homes and businesses and forcing folk to rebuild their lives from scratch. The town was now looking for leadership, which they found in John White, who inspired the leading citizens to take a radical look at the ordering of the town, including its provisions for social welfare. A hospital was founded for the care and education of the poorer children, almshouses were established for the needy elderly (these charities still continue today and one of the buildings, Nappers Mite, still stands in South Street), the provision of welfare payments for the poor and sick became a model of its kind, assisted by the establishment of a profitable business in a new municipal Brewery (which was also a means of controlling the sale of alcohol). The policing of both criminal and immoral activities was also tightened up. The mass of the population accepted and even came to welcome these reforms.

White himself gained an enthusiastic following, to hear him preach and lecture and attend the weekly biblical expositions – he went through the Bible from beginning to end in the course of six years and then again from the beginning. This lasted through to the time of the Civil War and up to his death in 1648. Benn was very much under his shadow for the whole of this period. The parish of All Saints was the poorer part of the town and relied on financial support from the other two, richer, parishes and this was reflected in the relationship between the two rectors. Part of Benn's ministry involved helping with services in the other churches.

John White also took the lead in the town in drawing up a covenant, known as the 'Ten Vows', which can be seen as a formal expression of the Puritan vision that motivated him and of a type which became common in this period. This covered such matters as the ordering of worship in church, the importance of reading and meditating on the Scriptures, and day-to-day godly living. All the people were called on to assent to this covenant, although John White was against excluding those who would not give their assent, in the hope that they would come round in time to such a commitment. William Benn followed a similar line to begin with but later came to regard those who had assented to the covenant as being a special group of the faithful within the wider congregation.

Generally the town resisted the efforts by King Charles I and Archbishop Laud to undo many of the changes introduced by the Puritans. When in 1633 Charles issued a declaration, known as the 'Book of Sports', which encouraged people to engage in recreation, such as dancing and archery, on Sundays as opposed to just during the week, White and Benn refused to read it out in church, as required. Local worthy, William Whiteway, in his diary records how the Bishop of Bristol took special steps to urge White, in particular, 'to read it before the Archbishop's Visitation, and upon his refusal, the Churchwardens in his absence procured Mr Holiday to read it on a Friday morning, 11 July, none being then at Church but he and the Clerk and the Churchwardens.' He goes on to comment that 'When Mr White heard of it he was exceeding angry', also that 'Mr Benn refused utterly to read it'. However, no action seems to have been taken against White or Benn as a consequence of this. The town also stopped theatrical productions, and travelling companies were banned from performing and told to leave the town. This was done even when their leader was able to produce a patent from the Master of the Revels, which authorised them to perform anywhere in the country.

Neither White nor Benn stuck slavishly to the Book of Common Prayer in conducting worship. In Benn's case one disgruntled parishioner said that he objected to passages in Benn's sermons and complained that his prayers were too long, he did not speak loud enough when giving names at christenings, and did not read the Common Prayer, the Commandments and Epistles and Gospels. Benn was generally thought to be somewhat long-winded. His son-in-law, Nathaniel Mather gave a more favourable assessment of him as 'a man so shining in holiness, so excelling in clearness of Gospel Light, and so abounding in solid, spiritual, practical, scriptural notions, that I have not known many that have gone beyond him, few that have equalled him'. A particular part of his ministry related to the town's Gaol, which was just down High East Street from All Saints Church at the corner with what is now Icen Way; Benn

King Charles I

Oliver Cromwell

was appointed chaplain and is said later to have arranged for the erection of a chapel at the Gaol.

When the Civil War broke out between King and Parliament Royalists noted the resolution and courage of Dorchester folk in support of Parliament and blamed the ministers for influencing the people in this direction. Both White and Benn ended up fleeing to London and supporting the Parliamentary cause from there, but this reflected the military situation of Dorchester rather than a shift in public opinion in the town. When asked how long the town's defences would withstand the Royalists a commander replied 'about half an hour'. After news arrived that Bristol had surrendered to the Royalists, Dorchester capitulated to an advancing force without a struggle.

Both White and Benn returned to Dorchester as soon as it was safe to do so. They found the town impoverished and they had to apply to Parliament's Committee for Plundered Ministers for financial assistance. The town failed to recover its former energy and enthusiasm. John White was now an old man and in failing health. He died in 1648 and Benn was left holding the fort until a new rector was appointed. This was Stanley Gower, in similar mould to John White, a Puritan but not holding extreme views; Benn was involved in assessing Gower's fitness for the post, so he does not appear to have been pushing for a more radical line at this stage.

Benn does not appear to have been a great supporter of the new rulers in London. When the Rump Parliament required all holders of municipal office take a new oath, the 'Engagement' to be 'true and faithful to the Commonwealth of England, as it is now established, without a King or House of Lords' Benn followed the example of some of the Dorchester worthies in subscribing 'in this sense only, that I will live peaceably under this present power and obey them in lawful things.' Nor was the town as a whole very keen on Oliver Cromwell: the collection on the Fast Day to commemorate

A cartoon of the time

Cromwell's death produced only £2.10s.0d from the parishes of St Peter's and Holy Trinity, with Benn's parish of All Saints showing a slightly warmer response of two pounds, perhaps a reasonable amount from such a poor parish.

Benn now felt able to exercise a freer hand in the ordering of his church and its worship. David Underdown's research found that no purchases of bread or wine are recorded throughout the 1650s, from which he concluded the sacrament of communion was never officially administered at All Saints during this period, communion presumably being restricted to 'the elect'. It is interesting to note that in 1655 Alice Limbury, a widow from Fordington, left money in her will to 'the church whereof I am a member in Dorchester'; she did not say 'parish' or give the name of a church, and she asked Benn to be one of her overseers. A committed Puritan, Philip Stansby, became mayor, and we will see later how he played a valuable role in supporting Benn and the new independent congregation, although he did not show similar support for the Baptists, who were refused permission to meet in any of the town's churches, nor, indeed. the Quakers, who were the most persecuted group of all.

Dorchester folk seem generally to have welcomed the Restoration in 1660, perhaps hoping for the return to a more orderly society after the upheavals of war and unstable government. There were also signs that the new Bishop of Bristol, Gilbert Ironside, was going to be reasonably accommodating. Some Cavaliers locally, however, took a number of Dorset ministers to court at the Assizes in September 1660 for not using the Anglican liturgy. Among them were William Benn and Joshua Churchill, minister at Fordington. Benn suffered a period of imprisonment, but did not lose his living at this stage.
As the new regime at Westminster sought to promote a more positively pro-Royalist agenda, the Corporation Act 1661 ordered the removal of all members of corporations who refused the oaths of supremacy and allegiance, would not receive the sacrament according to the rites of the Church of England, repudiate Parliament's 1643 oath of loyalty, the Solemn League and Covenant, and swear that it was unlawful 'upon any pretext whatsoever to take arms against the King'. Philip Stansby was among those who refused to repudiate the Covenant and he was expelled from the Corporation. Similar action was now taken against the clergy and we come to the Act of Uniformity, which required all ministers to take the same oath and declaration as in the Corporation Act and, specifically, to declare their loyalty to the re-established Church of England by St Bartholomew's Day, 24 August 1662. When the bishop conducted his visitation in September, neither Benn nor the Presbyterian-minded George Hammond, the current Rector of St Peter's and Holy Trinity, had done do. Action against Hammond was delayed until March the following year, perhaps in the hope that he might be persuaded to change his mind. Benn was not regarded so charitably, and on 10 September Bishop Ironside issued the 'intimation' removing him from the parish of All Saints. Benn clearly retained local support in the Town Clerk who managed to intercept it, and it was not delivered to the Apparitor, the appropriate officer of the ecclesiastical court, until 12 January 1663. A new rector, Richard Wine, arrived in February 1663. So Benn was formally ejected from his living.

Benn could no longer take services in All Saints Church, but there is evidence that a group of followers continued to meet with him as a 'gathered church'. When William Dry made his will in December 1663 he left ten shillings to Benn and the same amount to 'the poor of the church under his ministry of which I am a member'. The language clearly implies an identifiable group of worshippers, who can thus be reasonably identified as the beginnings of a Congregational Church in Dorchester. For a time this state of affairs seems to have been tolerated, except that individuals might be sent to gaol for breach of the obligation to attend worship within the Church of England. Even in gaol nonconformist worship continued. Renaldo Knapton, the Keeper of the Gaol, initially took a tolerant line, at least until he perceived that his tenure in his post might be threatened. He then took steps to stop sermons being preached in the Gaol, but it was still possible for clerical prisoners to be brought food and drink by their supporters and for baptisms etc to be conducted.

As to the reference to 'clerical prisoners' there were a number of nonconformist ministers in and around Dorchester. Several ejected ministers, including Benn, were rounded up and imprisoned in the aftermath of a nonconformist plot in Yorkshire, but most of them gave bonds for good behaviour and were released. This did not stop them remaining in Dorchester and carrying on as before but in a low key manner, meeting as 'conventicles' in private houses. In fact, David Underdown concluded from his research that 'Dorchester was the biggest nest of ejected ministers in the western counties, and few towns had so large and influential a dissenting community.' It may have been this fact that led the King to visit Dorchester in September 1665. The Court was then based in Salisbury, to escape the ravages of the plague in London, and the King took the opportunity to take a tour through Dorset. However, he chose Dorchester in particular to ceremonially give the royal assent to what is known as the 'Five Mile Act'. This prohibited nonconformist ministers who would not swear the oath of non-resistance from living within five miles of any corporate town (which would, of course, include Dorchester), or any place where they had previously held a living. George Hammond and Benjamin Way, both associated with St Peter's, and a few others took the oath and remained in Dorchester. William Benn moved to Maiden Newton, far enough to comply with the Act but still near enough to keep in touch with Dorchester. Of the two ejected from Fordington, Joshua Churchill went to Compton Valence, and Christopher Lawrence to Frampton.

It was not long before the exiled ministers drifted back into Dorchester. By 1669 Benn and Churchill were known to be preaching to a congregation in Fordington, not actually within the borough of Dorchester but clearly in breach of the Five Mile Act. Then, in 1672, came the Declaration of Indulgence which formally permitted nonconformists to worship publicly. In Dorchester and Fordington dissenting congregations were quickly licensed, one Presbyterian congregation served by George Hammond, and three Congregationalist fellowships, led respectively by William Benn, Joshua Churchill and Benjamin Way. William Benn's conventicle met in the home of Philip Stansby, the former Mayor of Dorchester. Joshua Churchill assisted Benn in Dorchester as well as being part of a conventicle in Fordington.

In this way the new gathered churches became established and, although the withdrawal of the Declaration of Indulgence let to a fresh bout of persecution, with leading dissenters such as Stansby being fined for being absent from their parish churches, the congregations continued to meet. Evidence for this is seen in a number of wills of the time. In 1671, for example, John Bartlett left two pounds each to a long list of dissenting clergy, including Benn, and James Palfrey, who died in 1673, did the same. Elizabeth Bedford left money for 'the poor of the society I belong to in

Dorchester'. Philip Stansby left two pounds to the poor of the congregation 'with whom I have walked in the fellowship of the Gospel'. Benn's involvement with the ministry at the Gaol seems to have continued, for it was in 1674 that the chapel was built within its walls, principally, we are told, 'at his own charge'.

Benn continued to minister into his old age. He is said to have been able to read without spectacles at the age of eighty, and to have prayed in his study seven times a day. He died in 1681 and was buried at All Saint's. Joshua Churchill put together a collection of his sermons and had them published under the title, Soul Prosperity, as a tribute to his memory, but Benn's real legacy was to be the continuing fellowship of dissenters, which would become formally known as Dorchester Congregational Church.

Dorchester United Church (formerly Congregational) as it is today.

Stourton Caundle Friendly Society

By Philip Knott

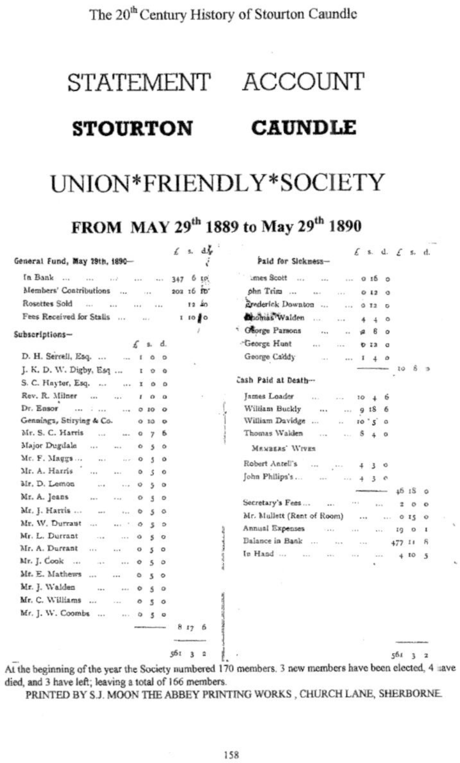

The 20th Century History of Stourton Caundle

STATEMENT ACCOUNT

STOURTON CAUNDLE

UNION*FRIENDLY*SOCIETY

FROM MAY 29th 1889 to May 29th 1890

	£ s. d.	£ s. d.
General Fund, May 29th, 1890—		
In Bank		347 6 10
Members' Contributions		202 16 10
Rosettes Sold		12 10
Fees Received for Stalls		1 10 0
Subscriptions—		
D. H. Serrell, Esq.	1 0 0	
J. K. D. W. Digby, Esq ...	1 0 0	
S. C. Hayter, Esq.	1 0 0	
Rev. R. Milner	1 0 0	
Dr. Ensor	0 10 0	
Gennings, Stirying & Co.	0 10 0	
Mr. S. C. Harris	0 7 6	
Major Dugdale	0 5 0	
Mr. F. Maggs	0 5 0	
Mr. A. Harris	0 5 0	
Mr. D. Lemon	0 5 0	
Mr. A. Jeans	0 5 0	
Mr. J. Harris	0 5 0	
Mr. W. Durrant	0 5 0	
Mr. L. Durrant	0 5 0	
Mr. A. Durrant	0 5 0	
Mr. J. Cook	0 5 0	
Mr. E. Mathews	0 5 0	
Mr. J. Walden	0 5 0	
Mr. C. Williams	0 5 0	
Mr. J. W. Coombs	0 5 0	
		8 17 6
		561 3 2

	£ s. d.	£ s. d.
Paid for Sickness—		
James Scott	0 16 0	
John Trim	0 12 0	
Frederick Downton	0 12 0	
Thomas Walden	4 4 0	
George Parsons	2 8 0	
George Hunt	0 12 0	
George Caddy	1 4 0	
		10 8 0
Cash Paid at Death—		
James Loader	10 4 6	
William Buckly	9 18 6	
William Davidge	10 5 0	
Thomas Walden	8 4 0	
Members' Wives		
Robert Antell's	4 3 0	
John Philips's	4 3 0	
		46 18 0
Secretary's Fees		2 0 0
Mr. Mullett (Rent of Room)		0 15 0
Annual Expenses		19 0 1
Balance in Bank		477 11 8
In Hand		4 10 5
		561 3 2

At the beginning of the year the Society numbered 170 members. 3 new members have been elected, 4 have died, and 3 have left; leaving a total of 166 members.

PRINTED BY S.J. MOON THE ABBEY PRINTING WORKS , CHURCH LANE, SHERBORNE.

158

The Stourton Caundle Friendly Society was formed in 1836, to which members contributed for sickness, unemployment and other misfortune. The scheme was financed by members' contributions, together and various fund raising activities. Any surplus funds were shared out between members on Oak Apple Day, celebrated on 29th of May each year, to commemorate the restoration of the monarchy in 1660. The three banners belonging to the society were paraded through the Village, finishing at the Tithe Barn in Court Barton Field. Any outstanding money from the previous year was then shared out between the members, and this was followed by a fete with tea and dancing.

The society's emblem, mounted on a large banner, was a skep bee-hive above clasped hands in the centre of a floral design, with bees, and a scroll bearing the inscription; 'May we all strive together like bees of a hive and never sting each other'. The fire-damaged banner was rescued from the 1971 hut fire and is now framed and mounted in the Village Hall.

Friendly Society procession 1922

Rules of the Stourton Caundle Slate Club.

1. **Name and Objects.** The Club shall be called the "STOURTON CAUNDLE SLATE CLUB," and is established for the purpose of affording mutual benefit for its members from year to year according to the following Rules. It is intended primarily for working men and women, and shall be under their management and control in conjunction with the Officers and Committee Members from time to time appointed.

The word "he" shall at all times be construed as meaning "he or she."

2. **Officers.** The Club shall be officered by a President, a Chairman, a Vice-Chairman and a Treasurer, the first to fulfil these Offices for the current year to be elected by the promotors and to be appointed for each subsequent year by members at each Annual General Meeting.

3. **Committee.** The promoters of the Club shall be its members, who shall appoint six of their number at least to act as their first Committee. The Committee for subsequent years shall be appointed at each Annual General Meeting.

4. **Trustees and Auditors.** The promoters shall elect two of its members to act as Trustees and two (not fulfilling any other Office) to act as Auditors. The members to fill these Offices shall hereafter be elected by members at each Annual General Meeting.

The successor to the Friendly Society was the Slate Club with an inaugural meeting held at Newleaze Farmhouse on 1st November 1935. A committee was elected and officers appointed by the forty parishioners who attended the meeting. Trustees and auditors were also appointed. The committee agreed that members could be accepted up to the age of fifty-five, and the committee would draft a set of rules for presentation to the next meeting. The proposed rules were presented to a meeting on 7th November and were passed with only minor amendments. The club organised fund-raising activities, such as whist drives and dances in the Village Hut. On 23rd August a Church Parade was organised, starting from the Jubilee Oak at 6pm, and headed by the standard bearers and the Boys Brigade Band from Sherborne, who had been engaged for the event at a fee of three pounds. The procession, including the Stalbridge Scout Group, paraded through the village, around the triangle, and returned to the cricket ground at the rear of Veales Cottage, for divine service at 7pm. The banners of the former Friendly Society had been repaired for the occasion, and a wooden case had been made in which to store them in the Young Men's clubroom.

Another procession was arranged for 11th August 1937. The Village Brass Band, formed for the Coronation celebrations in the May of that year, was at the head of the procession. The same route was followed as for the previous year, and after the procession the Reverend Fincher officiated at an open-air service at which hymns were sung accompanied by the band.

The AGM and share-out of money took place in December each year, and the club continued to flourish through the war years with membership steady at well over one hundred, including members from Stalbridge, Stalbridge Weston and Thornhill. However, national and local social conditions changed considerably in the years immediately following WW2, especially with the introduction of the NHS, and the club's importance gradually diminished, with it finally disbanding in 1950.

The Village Band-
Standing: William Guy, Ambrose Stainer, ? James Guy, Vernon Guy, ?, Dennis Furnell, Albert Light, Frank Palmer, Reg Lane, Bill Stainer, Jim Ashford, George Furnell.
Kneeling: ?, Bob Ashford, Bob Green, Harold Brown, Walter Hays.

The Stourton Caundle Slate Club

Balance Sheet 1939

RECEIPTS.	£	s.	d.
Entrance Fees		6	0
Cards		7	4
112 Members at 26/-	145	12	0
2 ,, lapsed		8	0
Fines		2	6
Death Levy	2	16	0
Entertainment	4	15	6
Honorary Subscription—			
Mr. Fernandes	1	1	0
Mr. Matthews		10	0
Balance from 1938	13	1	8
	£169	0	0

EXPENDITURE.	£	s.	d.
Sick Pay—			
Sis. A. Lillington	4	0	0
,, M. Lane	4	0	0
,, V. Bealing	2	3	4
,, M. Dennett		18	4
,, J. Kirby	2	5	0
,, E. Lake	3	1	8
Bro. A. Light	7	10	0
,, W. Brown	2	0	0
,, J. Knight	1	13	4
,, A. Walden	1	10	0
,, S. Jeans	1	10	0
,, J. Harding	1	10	0
,, J. Stainer		11	8
,, M. Knight		10	0
,, L. Lake		10	0
,, L. Jeans		10	0
Death Levy	2	16	0
Printing		18	0
Cheques		5	0
Hire of Hut	1	10	0
Secretary's Fee	5	14	0
112 Members @ £1	112	0	0
Balance	11	18	8
	£169	0	0

Audited and found Correct—A. M. HOLDWAY, E. M. GOULD

H. J. HOLDWAY, Hon. Treasurer. C. J. ORCHARD, Secretary.

HUGH C. PARSONS, STALBRIDGE

The Annual General Meeting and share out of money, took place in the December of each year. The Club continued throughout the war years with membership steady at well over one hundred, with some members from Stalbridge Weston, Stalbridge and Thornhill. The Club finally disbanded in 1950, after the introduction of the National Health Service.

The banners were paraded through the village for the last time at the head of the 1953 Coronation Parade. Betty Toone is holding the accordion. Wearing sashes, from left to right, are Harry Holdway, Bob Ashford and Cecil Orchard.

Local Highway Maintenance in the Inter-War Years

By Philip Knott

Until the late 1920s minor road surfaces were uneven and, in summertime, very dusty. Sturminster Rural District Council was responsible for the maintenance of the roads located within its district council area, and a small gang of roadmen was based locally. This gang maintained a defined length of roadway in and around each parish, with the man in charge referred to as the Lengths-Man. The men took a pride in their work, keeping the roads and paths clear of weeds and dirt, digging the roadside ditches, patching potholes, trimming the grass banks and verges and clearing blocked drains.

The 1920s Sturminster Road Gang

The stone used for road building and repairs in the parish of Stourton Caundle was excavated from a quarry at Garvey, adjoining Caundle Lane, near the parish boundary with Bishops Caundle. Iron bars and sledge-hammers were used to break out the rock. The Quarrymen were paid on piecework for every square yard of stone excavated, and they were paid a day rate for removal of topsoil prior to commencement of quarrying. The stone was loaded by shovels into horse-drawn putts, and hauled to where ever it was required by Robert (Bob) Green, who was contracted to the district council. Bob stabled his horses at the rear of the

Trooper Inn where his parents were the licensees. The stone was then cracked to the required size and placed in position on the road surface for compaction by means of a Clayton and Shuttleworth steam-roller, owned by the RDC. This roller had previously been used by the army during WW1 and must have come close to being destroyed by enemy action, judging by the dents incurred on its chimney as a result of enemy shrapnel.

On arrival the driver would climb down from the footplate and carry out routine maintenance of the engine, ensuring that everything was ready for the next morning when an early fire would be needed to heat the boiler.

Members of the maintenance gang in the Sturminster Newton area.

Local government reorganisation in 1928 resulted in the transfer of responsibility for all highways maintenance to Dorset County Council. Tarmac surfacing of minor roads then followed. The wide verge opposite the cemetery in Drove Road was the engine driver's chosen spot for parking his steam-roller, van and water cart. A few days before work was due to start, loads of gravel and steam coal were deposited at the nearest suitable location. Then one evening the steamroller would arrive, towing a caravan and water barrel. On arrival the driver would climb down

The caravan provided very basic living accommodation. Access was by means of wooden steps attached to the doorway, an enamel bowl, soap and towel with steaming water drawn from the engine's boiler provided washing facilities. Through the open door the driver could be seen lighting the fire in the small range-type grate. A small cupboard door was opened and a kettle, teapot, caddy and mug taken out, followed by a frying pan, fat, eggs and bacon rashers. During the evening, boys of all ages would arrive in Drove Road to chat with the driver and to listen, enthralled, to his tales of what it was like to lead such a nomadic life. Transfixed by his experiences with the many different steam-rollers he had driven and where he had been working, reciting a list of village names which to the boys present seemed to be far reaching and exotic but were of course all located within a few miles of home.

Next morning saw the arrival of the horse-drawn tarring machine, belching smoke from its boiler and carrying the smell of boiling tar. With its metal wheels, smoking stack, tar barrel sitting on top, and all its spraying attachments, to us youngsters it was quite awesome! The men, with their big heavy boots, had a system which worked without a hitch. Starting with spraying-on the steaming liquid tar, which was forced through a lance spray by means of a hand pump, requiring two men to operate it. The liquid tar was transported in barrels which were collected by horse and cart from Stalbridge station. The barrel was hauled by a purpose-built horse putt, with a coal fire underneath to heat and emulsify the liquid tar prior to spraying. The putt was constructed with quick-release shafts to free the horses should the tar catch fire. Then the gravel, delivered by lorry from Warmwell Quarry, was scattered by hand shovels on to the liquid tar before being steam-rolled under the expert hands of the friendly engine driver.

The weekly wage for the road men during the 1930s, was £1.12s.0d, with an additional allowance of one shilling per week for the provision of a pedal cycle to ride to work. From the late 1940s tarmacadam was introduced for road surfacing. This was delivered by lorry from the Mendip quarries and dropped off in heaps along the roadway for spreading by hand shovels, and compaction by a diesel powered road roller, much as it is today.

Tarmac Surface Dressing in Stourton Caundle High Street in the 1930s.

Louis Arbon Strange

Rev. Dr. John Travell

"Flying Rebel" is the title Group Captain Peter Hearn gave to his official biography of Louis Arbon Strange, a Dorset Farmer's boy who became a brilliant pilot and made his own distinctive and substantial contribution to the successful outcome of two world wars.

In the Dorset and Devon's Military Museum, at the Keep in Dorchester, they have on display the remarkable group of medals that were awarded to this extraordinary man, who sadly, has largely been forgotten. Not many of those who visit the Museum would be aware of his outstanding military career. Louis Arbon Strange was one of the generation whose fate it was to be called to serve in two world wars, just twenty years apart, and he rose to the demands and challenges of those terrible years with indomitable courage and exceptional distinction in both.

A Most Distinguished Set of Medals
Photo: Trevor Mathews

DSO, OBE, MC, DFC & Bar, 1914 Star with Front-Line Clasp, WW1 War Medal, WW1 Victory Medal with MiD Oak Leaf, 1939-45 Star, Aircrew Europe Star with France/Germany Bar, WW2 Defence Medal, WW2 War Medal & American Bronze Star.

Recently, Peter Metcalfe, who is a military historian at the Keep, who did know his story, realised that Louis, who survived both wars, and whose family were farmers in the Purbecks near Worth Matravers, must have been buried somewhere near there, and with Captain Colin Parr, the former curator of the Museum, went searching for his grave. They succeeded in finding it, in the burial ground of the Norman St. Nicholas parish church of the village.

The headstone was in a row of similar memorials, with nothing to distinguish it, and was in a very weather-worn condition, and the inscription was barely readable. With the help of a local stonemason they had it restored, and felt that now this had been done, Louis Strange should not continue to be forgotten and his grave neglected, and so, with the ready support of the Vicar of the parish, James John Mercer, they arranged a service of re-dedication and remembrance, which took place at the graveside on Saturday, 27 July, which was also the date on which Louis was born in 1891. Colin Parr had made contact with members of Strange's family and a large number of them came together from all over the country as well as from Scotland and France to the service, which was also attended by representatives of the Dorset Yeomanry, the Regiment and the Royal Air Force, who laid wreaths on the grave.

Louis Strange was born at Keyneston Mill, in Tarrant Keyneston, in the Stour valley, where his family had been farmers for several generations. As soon as he was old enough, he followed the family tradition and joined the Dorsetshire

Yeomanry as a trooper at Blandford Camp. In 1910 he watched the Bournemouth Flying Display and was fascinated by the idea of flying. He made a bet with his fellow troopers that he would fly over their camp the following year. Then, having been injured in a farming accident, he learnt to fly, and gained his Royal Aero Club Certificate at Hendon in 1913. Having become the fifth member of the exclusive 'Upside-down Club' who had looped the loop in one of those flimsy early flying machines, he joined the Central Flying School at Upavon, and was commissioned as a second lieutenant in the Dorsetshire Regiment in July, 1914, just five days before war was declared with Germany. He was posted to the 5th. Squadron of the Royal Flying Corps and flew to Amiens on 16 August, 1914.

Strange as a Junior Officer in the Royal Flying Corps
Photo: Trevor Matthews

At this time aircraft were not thought of as war machines but only as useful for reconnaissance but Strange had the imagination and intelligence to anticipate the role aircraft would come to play and was the first British pilot to have a Lewis gun fitted to his Farman Biplane. To begin with, Strange's job was to fly over the enemy troops and report their movements to the British Army forces on the ground. But seeing the German troops below him, he and his observer made up three petrol bombs and attacked the German transport near St. Quentin. But, in December, as the rest of his squadron were busy opening their hampers and gifts on the first Christmas Day of the War, he took off alone in his plane to fly over the German airfield and dropped them a football.

In 1915 he was promoted to Captain and became a flight commander. He was awarded a Military Cross for leading a bombing mission on the German trains in the railway station at Courtrai. This was the first time that planes had been sent on a bombing raid as part of a battle plan.

Then he had the incredible 'Boys' Own Paper' adventure that more than anything else revealed his strength of character and his refusal to be defeated. Flying his Martinsyde Scout at 8,500 feet above the Menin Ridge chasing a German plane, his Lewis gun jammed as he changed the ammunition. He stood up in the cockpit and held the control stick with his knees while he tried to release the gun. But the plane flipped over upside-down. His safety belt broke as he fell out of the cockpit without a parachute. He clung on to the ammunition drum of his Lewis as the plane flew towards the ground. He managed to swing his legs up into the cockpit and with his feet, he wiggled the control column and fell back into the cockpit as he flipped the plane over again and piloted it safely to the ground. When he landed, he was criticised by his commanding officer for 'causing unnecessary damage' to his instrument

Strange Dangling from his Up-turned Martinsyde Scout.

(See Editor's Note for Copyright)

panel and the cockpit seat in his efforts to get back into the plane.

In November, 1915, he married Marjorie Beath, the young girl he had given a ride in his plane before the War. His best man was another air ace, Major Lanoe Hawker, V.C. Strange, who by then had become the longest serving officer in the Royal Flying Corps, was promoted to Major and posted to Gosport to form 23 Squadron. The present squadron briefing room opened in 1997, is named after him. Strange next formed No.1 School of Air Gunnery at Hythe in Kent. Then, promoted to Lieutenant-Colonel, he formed No.2 School of Air Gunnery at Turnberry. In April he took over from Hugh Trenchard, (now remembered as the Father of the RAF), as the Assistant Commandant of the Central Flying School, where he insisted on testing all the new flying machines himself. He went back into action in June 1918 to take charge of the new 80th Wing, with seven squadrons under his command, two of which were Australian. During the next five months he was awarded both the Distinguished Flying Cross and the Distinguished Service Order for his development, planning and leading of co-ordinated big-wing fighter-bomber attacks on German airfields. Sadly, his younger brother, who was also an air ace, was shot down and killed in September, 1918.

Between the Wars strange became the chief flying instructor at Upavon and then commanded the flying wing of the RAF College at Cranwell, considered 'the most prestigious flying appointment in the service.' Serving under him, as his Administration Officer, was Squadron Leader Charles Portal (later to become Marshal of the RAF the Viscount Portal and wartime Chief of the Air Staff). In 1922 Strange retired from the RAF because of ill health, and returned to Dorset to work on the farm his father had bought at Worth Matravers. The RAF then had no provision for retired ranks, so he resigned his commission and retired as a Lieutenant-Colonel in the Dorsetshire Regiment. But he couldn't give up flying, and became co-director with Oliver Simmonds, an ex- Supermarine aircraft designer, to form Simmonds Aircraft Ltd. with Strange as the chief test pilot of all their new aircraft. He flew in many of the air races that were popular in the 1920s and 30s, including the King's Cup and the international air shows where the latest new planes were exhibited. In October 1928, he flew to Berlin. In 1930 his company became part of Saunders Roe, making variations of their Spartan aircraft. Then, in 1935, the company was merged with Hillman Airways and United Airlines – which eventually became British Airways, and Louis left to team up with Whitney Straight, an American Anglophile racing car driver, to form the Straight Corporation Ltd. To meet the need of more pilots for the growing number of passenger airline companies, Straight formed Straight Aviation Training Ltd. and Strange became again involved in teaching pilots to fly. In 1936, as the fear of another war grew, the RAF started sending men to civilian flying schools for instruction, and all Strange's skill and experience were needed once more.

When the next war started in 1939, the Straight Corporation was immediately taken over by the government to provide air transport to carry military personnel and goods in England and France. Aged 49, Strange was too old for a regular commission so he joined the RAF Volunteer Reserve as a Pilot Officer and was posted to the RAF's Transport and Communications Squadron. In May 1940 he was sent to Merville in France to take over as the Squadron Control Officer with orders to save what was left of their planes as the Germans advanced. With the enemy only 500 yards away, Strange climbed into the only Hurricane left to escape back to Britain. This plane had been badly damaged; it was there for repairs and had most of its instruments missing and all its guns removed. And it was a plane he had never flown before. As he flew off, he was spotted by a squadron of six Messerschmitt 109s who chased him at tree top height along village streets until he got clear and over the sea, where a Royal Navy ship fired its guns at the Messerschmitts and drove them away. For this Strange was awarded a bar to the DFC he had been awarded in the First World War, making him the only pilot to receive this medal in the two World Wars.

Promoted to Squadron Leader, he was sent to Ringway near Manchester for parachute training and became commander of the Central Landing School. Winston Churchill was determined to develop airborne troops which the Germans had proved to be very effective. He visited Ringway and met Strange there in April 1941. Strange put on a demonstration drop of 140 parachutists for Churchill to see. He took the opportunity to speak with Churchill on his own, and Churchill took quick action to see that Strange received all the support and resources he needed, and the many more soldiers that were needing to be trained. This was the U.K.'s only parachute training unit, and pioneered the parachute training system for all the allied airborne forces. Using the techniques developed by Strange over 60,000 allied paratroopers were trained there between 1940 and 1946.

Strange was next appointed to MSFU – the Merchant Ships Fighter Unit, which fitted fighter aircraft on to ships so that they could be catapulted off to combat the German Condor long range bombers which were attacking the Atlantic convoys.

About fifty Hurricanes, known as Hurricats, were adapted and set out with the convoys. Whether training men to jump out of aeroplanes or to be catapulted into the air by rockets off ships at sea, with every group of new recruits Strange always went first, to show them how to do it and to boost their confidence. By 1942 the Condor threat had been defeated and the Hurricats were moved to the Gibraltar convoys. Having succeeded in its task, the MSFU was formally disbanded in July 1943.

In December he was appointed to 46 Group as Wing Commander of a special transport group, planning operations in preparation for the D. Day landings on 6 June 1944. Flying back to his base at Netheravon, under heavy cloud which

Strange as an RAF Wing Commander.

obscured landmarks, he was forced down into a narrow valley. Unable to see the airfield he told his companion to 'Look out for Fresians." 'Friesian what?' he was asked. "Cows' said Louis. Coming in sight of some cows he was told 'There they are." Taking a look, Louis said 'You fool, those are Herefords, Fresians are black and white.' A little later, seeing the Fresians, Louis immediately lifted the plane straight up into the cloud and came through it on to the landing strip. 'Do you always navigate by cows?" he was asked. 'Not at milking time.' he said. Having trained the pilots and prepared the flying crews and airborne troops for D.Day, he flew as crew himself in the lead Dakota aircraft to drop the first parachutists before the beach invasion began. He landed in Normandy himself on 15 June to establish temporary staging posts for landing supplies as the troops advanced. He quickly had six airstrips under his control to defend the beachhead. His fleet of Dakotas flew in supplies and flew back with the wounded; over 50,000 of them in the next three months.

He was also in control of local administration as the allies advanced. In October 1944 he was with the H.Q. of the 1st Allied Airborne Army, comprising four American and two British Airborne Divisions. He was appointed as Deputy Chief of Staff to the American General in charge, who could not believe that with all his medals, his record and his experience he was no more than a Wing Commander. Saying that 'if he was an American, he would have been a General', he persuaded a reluctant RAF to give him temporary promotion as Acting Group Captain. (This was the highest rank he ever attained in the RAF.)

Strange's habit of cutting through red tape and ignoring official channels and proper procedures in fulfilling all the important and demanding tasks he was given, and making them efficient and operational in the shortest possible time, regularly offended his superior officers, but those who knew him and had served with him and under him in both World Wars had the highest respect and warmest regard for him. Several of those he had taught and commanded in the First World War had attained high rank in the Second. They still remembered him with affection as Strange now found himself serving under them. One of these, the Air Commodore who was then Louis' Commanding Officer of 46 Group, wrote to thank him for his success in training airborne troops in time for D-Day. He said, 'I am deeply grateful to you. I would again serve under you most willingly.' Writing in 1965, Harry Cobby, an Australian who had flown alongside him in 1918, wrote about him. 'He was a grand type, both as a man and a leader of flying people.' The aviation historian Richard Thownsend Bickers, described meeting him in 1942: 'He was very popular and admired...he exuded exuberant energy and a strong, attractive personality...Louis Strange was one of the most electrifying personalities I ever met; only Douglas Bader made the same instant forceful impact.' And those he had trained to fly Hurricanes of ships at sea said, 'It was an experience serving under him. He was above all, human and kind, but quite dotty.'

Towards the end of the War he was made an OBE and took charge of Advance Headquarters, 46 Group, to form a new squadron and to expand existing squadrons and train them for Airborne Force Operations. For this work he was awarded a Bronze Star by the Americans., the citation for which said, 'Wing Commander Strange rendered a major contribution to the successful accomplishment of Airborne Operations against the enemy during the period, 14 December 1944 until the cessation of hostilities in Europe'.

Strange was present at SHAEF Headquarters in Reims to witness the end of these hostilities with the surrender of the German Forces to Montgomery on 4 May 1945 . After the War he returned to Worth Matravers and to his farm. He couldn't stop flying, and bought himself a small Auster plane and flew in several competitions. He re-established his links

The Rev Dr John Travell officiating at the Service of Re-dedication and Remembrance.

Photo by: Trevor Matthews

with civilian aviation becoming the managing director of the Hampshire School of Flying and the Hants. Aero Club. In 1947 he was the guest speaker at the first Annual Dinner of the Dorchester Branch of the RAF Association. He enjoyed flying to re-unions of his former squadrons where he was always a welcome and honoured guest. In 1956 he was given the Freedom of the Guild of Air Pilots and Air Navigators. Flying to Germany in 1957 to attend the disbandment of No.5 Squadron, with whom he had fought in 1914, he took the controls of a Vampire jet, having made his first flight in a flimsy canvas and wire and wood-strutted biplane from Blandford Downs in 1911.

But increasingly ill health was limiting his activities. He had never been physically robust and had been seriously ill with the flu epidemic in 1919. He suffered from painful, disabling bouts of sciatica and his poor health meant that he was unable to continue in some posts as long as might have been expected. Suffering physically and mentally and worn out by war, he died in Poole in November, 1966, aged 75. He left his medals to the Keep Military Museum in Dorchester where they are on permanent display.

Louis Strange's Restored Headstone at Worth Matravers
Photo by Trevor Matthews

The moving service which Colin Parr and Peter Metcalfe had arranged at his grave beside the church at Worth Matravers, which they had rediscovered and had restored, attracted a great deal of attention in the national press, so that Louis' name and achievements are now known to the readers of these newspapers who, on seeing the accounts of his exploits, have expressed their astonishment in the correspondence columns that they had never heard of him before. But here, in his own county, this son of Dorset, whose real deeds far outdid those of the fictional Biggles, should continue to be proudly remembered and h hat he was so proud to join.

Editor's Note. Together with the RAF Museum, TSO Ltd and others we have attempted, without success, to trace the artist of the drawing of Louis Strange dangling from his WW1 aeroplane. If the legal copyright holders ever wish to contact us we shall ensure that correct acknowledgement appears in any future edition of this book.

The William Barnes Society

The Beauty of Blackmore

Portrait of William Barnes

By Marion Tate

Close your eyes, relax and let your mind take you to the sights, sounds and aromas of the beautiful Blackmore Vale. Imagine rich meadow lands, bound with verdant hedgerows, rolling hills and woodlands, and well-worn footpaths. Picture cattle grazing, lambs gambolling, farmers making hay: 'We haymeakers, in snow white sleeves, do work in 'sheades o' quiv'ren leaves'. Contemplate streams glistening and playing over stones, the abundance of clotes – yellow waterlilies. See pools, shallows and rivers meandering their way onwards: Stour, Frome, Caundle and Lydden Brook. Listen to the voices of children playing, the loud peals of church bells carried on the air, birds singing and the excitement of the seasonal markets and fayres. Breathe in the smell of the damp earth, green grasses, hay drying, river banks, wild flowers, sweet wild wroses, wild honeyzucks

Bagber Common ***Photo Jonathan North***

a'vound, primwrose, cowslips and animal dung. Each season brings a new palette of colours and changes the mood of this spectacular landscape.

The Dorset Poet, William Barnes, was born in the Blackmore Vale on February 22nd 1801 at Rush-Hay a small farmling at Bagber near Sturminster Newton. He was the fifth child of at least six children born to Grace and John Barnes. Though William's grandfather had been a prosperous yeoman, his father was recorded in the census of Sturminster Newton as "Labourer in Husbandry". John Barnes's livelihood was barely above subsistence level and the family lived in a poor thatched cottage.

Barnes was an extremely intelligent child and had a passion for books and learning. He loved the Vale with a passion and it was his use of the language and his awareness and retention of the sights and sounds of the working-class people in the area which inspired his dialect poetry.

Barnes attended a dame's school in Sturminster Newton followed by a Church school nearby. It was his splendid handwriting which gained him his first employment as a copy-clerk for Thomas Dashwood, the local solicitors.

Four years later Barnes became an engrossing clerk with the firm of Thomas Coombs & Son, Dorchester. He now lived and worked in the prosperous town of Dorchester. He taught himself engraving, played the organ, flute, violin and continued his study of languages. In all, he taught himself to converse in 70 different languages.

It was here in Dorchester that Barnes fell in love with Julia Miles as she stepped down from a Magnet stagecoach in the cobbled yard of the King's Arms Hotel. Barnes was 18 and Julia 14. Julia's parents opposed him as a suitor on the grounds of poverty. They even curtailed chaperoned meetings. Their courtship lasted 9 years.

An early piece that Barnes wrote to his love:

TO JULIA

The sun again sets, and the moon in his room,
Illumines once more the bright waves of the Frome;
But who sails upon it? for our slender oar
Shall trouble its transparent waters no more.
O think on the Frome, love! And give me a sigh
For the hours that are past, for the pleasures gone by.

It was during this time that Barnes decided to embark on a new career - teaching. He needed to impress Julia's parents that he was worthy of their daughter's hand in marriage.

After keeping a school in Mere, Wiltshire, for several years he obtained approval from her father to marry Julia. The ceremony took place at the parish church of Nailsea, Bristol in 1827. His beloved Julia had become his wife, the woman who was to be a source of intense happiness and a devoted support to him as long as she lived.

William Barnes's career as a much loved and successful schoolmaster covered almost forty years. Firstly, as schoolmaster in Mere and then in Dorchester where he opened three schools. Many of his pupils went on to become men of standing, such as Sir Frederick Treves surgeon to Edward V11 and Queen Victoria, Benjamin Fossett Locke who became a judge. His concerns with those too poor to seek legal representation led ultimately to the modern Legal Aid Scheme.

During these years Julia and Barnes had raised a family of seven children. When Julia died, in 1852, Laura, the eldest daughter, took over the role as mother. She devoted her life to caring for her father until he, too, died in 1886.

For the last 24 years of his life, Barnes was a minister. He had the great happiness to be presented to the living of Winterborne Came and Whitcombe. From Came Rectory he looked after his parishioners well and was loved by all. He also set up a school for farmworkers' children and started a Sunday choir with the support of his daughters.

Many literary figures made the pilgrimage to Came Rectory when Barnes was rector, including: Alfred Lord Tennyson, Prince Louis Lucien Bonaparte, Allingham, Patmore, Palgrave, Quiller-Couch, Gosse and his mentee, Thomas Hardy.

Barnes never forgot his roots. His love for the Blackmore Vale and the ordinary people never wavered. He loved nature and was content among the water meadows of Cloty Stour, the harvest fields of Dorset and was well aware of the solace which nature can bring to a sorrowful heart. But the people were always more important to him. He was always a man for the people, evidenced in part by the mainstay of his poetry, written in the Dorset dialect. Barnes wrote over 600 dialect poems and over 200 in National English.

Photo of John Blackmore

Through his poetry, Barnes has left us an amazing legacy. We have a fascinating insight into a rural way of life of a bygone era that could have been so easily lost in time: preserving an endangered culture of Old Dorset.

It portrays the beauty of the Blackmore Vale, its people, customs and culture and rural employment before mechanisation: traditional life slowly giving way to the modern age.

The Beauty of Blackmore

John Blackmore is a 26-year-old singer, song-writer, poet and teacher from Somerset.

John discovered William Barnes whilst studying English Literature at university and wrote his undergraduate dissertation on the dialect poet, exploring how music, specifically folk music, might be a means of bringing Barnes's poetry back to popularity and public consciousness. Ralph Vaughan Williams's setting of Linden Lea was an obvious place to start. John explored the possibility of setting other works to music and arranging them for voice and guitar. John was a semi-finalist in the 2011 BBC Radio 2 Young Folk Award competition. His musical settings of William Barnes's poetry were given a wider audience in 2014 when he contributed to the BBC Radio 4 documentary "Dorset Rewritten" about William Barnes.

Since then John has been working with the William Barnes Society on his latest album, 'Beauty of Blackmore'. The name comes from one of his compositions in praise of this very special part of the world. John is very excited to bring this Dorset literary figure to a new audience and allow those familiar with Barnes a new perspective on his work. He is thrilled to see his original works alongside his arrangements of Barnes's poems offering a perspective of rural life in south-west England today.

Music is a wonderful medium and 'Beauty of Blackmore' offers the opportunity to reinforce our wonderful cultural heritage left to us by William Barnes magnificent portrayal of the Vale in verse. It will offer opportunities for William Barnes and other west country writing to reach wider and younger audiences.

Until recently John was Head of Faculty for English and Drama at a secondary school in Wincanton. Although He loves teaching, as Barnes did, now is his time to follow his passion for Barnes, music and poetry. From September he will be working on a three-year programme towards his PhD. He has been awarded a studentship through The South West and Wales Doctoral Training Partnership, and he is hoping to gain a better understanding of Barnes by considering the interrelationship between his eclectic writings.

He is interested, too, in exploring how Barnes's writing continues to shape notions of regional and national rural identity in the twenty-first century and how an holistic understanding of Barnes offers new opportunities to encounter his work. Over the coming months he is assisting Professor Tom Burton (University of Adelaide) and Professor Emma Mason (University of Warwick) with research for a scholarly collection of Barnes's poetry that was first published in the Dorset County Chronicle.

John Blackmore is a talented young man who is actively engaged as a member of the William Barnes Society, bringing his own style of music and song to Outreach events as well as Events programme.

We wish John well with his studying. He is a real asset to the Society and we are proud of him. A little bird has told me that William Barnes is too!

(Editor's Note: Most of our members and other readers will be well aware of the huge contribution made by Dorset's William Barnes to both our national and local literature. Barnes's work and life have been aptly outlined in this entertaining and informative article by Marion who is the Honorary Secretary to The William Barnes Society.
This Dorchester-based society draws its membership from those who admire the work of William Barnes and who celebrate and promote it through a busy annual programme of meetings, recitals, outreach events and other activities which seek to engage new generations in Barnes's legacy. These activities are held in both Dorchester and at Winterbourne Came, where Barnes was rector of St. Peter's Church from 1862 until his death in 1886, and also at other locations around the County where the Society takes part in significant local events.

Dave Burbidge reciting a poem.

John Tait laying a wreath at memorial statue.

Those who would like to participate in these events or join the Society should call-up the Society's website "The William Barnes Society".

The Powys Society

Chris Thomas

On Saturday 30 March 2019 we celebrated the 50th anniversary of the Powys Society at a special event hosted by Corpus Christi College, Cambridge, the alma mater of the Powys family. As early as 1967 a small group of Powys enthusiasts had held discussions about the possibility of founding a Society dedicated to the Powyses. But it was not until 1969 that we were officially constituted as a Society with a committee and Chairman aimed at promoting wider recognition of the important contribution of the Powyses to English literature. From its earliest days the Society has been privileged to be associated with distinguished figures from the world of academic learning and literature such as Professor George Steiner, Fellow of Churchill College, Cambridge, the novelist Angus Wilson, the literary critic G Wilson Knight and the poet Kenneth Hopkins, all of whom have kindly lent the Society their great support and encouragement enabling us to become established.

Oil Painting by Gertrude Powys

At our anniversary event generous tributes were paid to our current long serving President, Glen Cavaliero, poet and literary critic, who described a trip he made in 1958 to visit John Cowper Powys (then in his 86th year) at his home in Wales. Glen read passages to us from his contemporary diary recording this memorable event. Tributes were also paid to all our past officials, volunteers, and the many contributors to our publications. David Goodway, our current Vice-Chairman, gave a brief account of how the Powys Society was formed.

The event provided us with an opportunity to reflect seriously on our history and celebrate our successes over a long period. Our Newsletter, the Powys Review and the Powys Journal provide an impressive collection of informed articles from a wide variety of scholars testifying to the deep interest in the works of the Powyses over 50 years. We were delighted to welcome to our event Lucy Hughes, archivist of Corpus Christi, who showed us many rare documents, photos, letters and other items relating to the Powyses at Cambridge. It was an honour and a privilege to visit Corpus Christi, take lunch in the impressive college dining hall, observe the location of the rooms occupied by John

Cowper and Llewelyn Powys when they were students here, and explore places in Cambridge associated with members of the Powys family in the company of a group of sympathetic enthusiasts.

Society members dining at Corpus Christy College, Cambridge

For over three hundred years there have been close connections between Corpus Christi College and Dorset. In 1697 Thomas Tenison (1636-1715), Archbishop of Canterbury,

1695-1715, purchased the perpetual advowson of the living of Stalbridge which he subsequently bequeathed "for ever" to the Masters, Fellows and Scholars of Corpus Christi College. The Masters' History of the College of Corpus Christi by John Lamb (1835) pronounces that "Stalbridge is considered one of the best livings in the county of Dorset." Littleton Charles Powys (1791-1872), John Cowper's paternal grandfather, was Rector of Stalbridge from 1837 to 1866. Littleton had a successful career at Cambridge – he was Fellow of Corpus Christi from 1814 to 1837, and Junior Proctor from 1822 to 1823. But when he decided to marry Amelia Knight (1802-1890) in 1838 he was required to leave his post at the college. As Bursar he was able to award himself "the richest living the College held." Littleton's son, and John Cowper's father, Charles Francis Powys (1843-1923), later vicar of Montacute in Somerset, was born in Stalbridge and continued the family tradition by attending Corpus Christi College. Llewelyn Powys, movingly describes in an essay entitled Stalbridge Rectory, how his father in his old age disappeared one day and attempted to reconnect with his boyhood home by walking from Templecombe to Stalbridge hoping to meet his childhood family "clothed again in the sweet flesh of life, united and happy in those dreaming rooms of the ancient Rectory of Stalbridge in Dorset."

Later in the year we celebrated another anniversary. 2019 marked ninety years since the first publication of one of John Cowper Powys's most popular and successful novels – Wolf Solent - which can still be found in print published by Penguin Modern Classics.

The Powys Society committee held a meeting in June at Sherborne Preparatory

School where some members of the Powys family were pupils. John Cowper describes in his Autobiography how he suffered at school where he was relentlessly bullied. After our meeting committee members were invited by Sherborne School archivist, Rachel Hassall to visit the School archives and library where we examined documents and photos and studied original information relating to the famous Sherborne Pageant of 1905 (surely a model for the pageant in John Cowper's novel A Glastonbury Romance?) in which William Powys (1888-1978) took a part. William was the youngest of the Powys brothers and attended the school between 1902 and 1906. He later went on to manage a farm in East Africa. Sherborne school features in Wolf Solent as do other prominent landmarks of the town (called Ramsgard in Powys's novel), including the Abbey, the Castle, the Pageant gardens (called the public gardens), the Digby Hotel (the Lovelace Hotel) and also, most memorably, as Powys described in a later preface to the novel, all the "hills and valleys, the trees and various flowers, the lanes and hedges and ponds and ditches of the country round Sherborne". Wolf Solent was written whilst Powys was in America, He called it, appropriately, "a book of nostalgia".

which she entitled Perdita Wane after one of the leading characters. We were delighted to launch Jacqueline's translation at our conference and offer copies of her book to members. The book cover shows a scene on Weymouth beach below the Jubilee clock photographed sometime between 1890 and 1900.

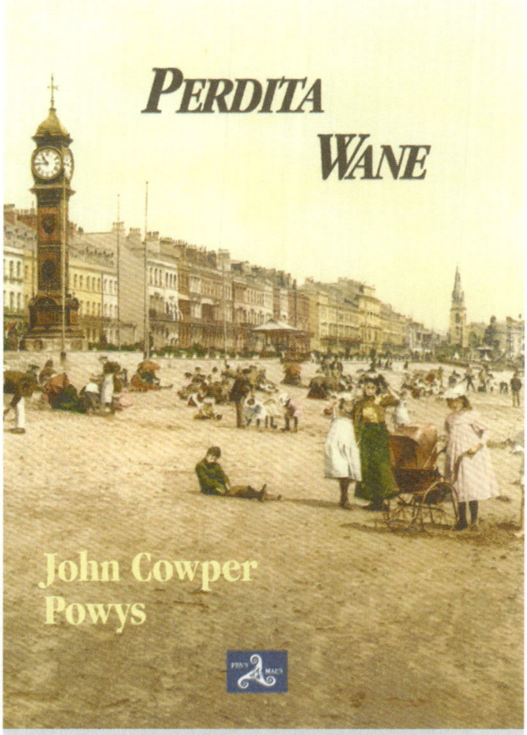

Front Cover of Perdita Wane

Our annual conference, held in Wales, in Llangollen was saddened by news of the death of one of our most passionately committed Powys enthusiasts, Jacqueline Peltier in Brittany who translated several books by John Cowper into French and founded and edited a bi- lingual journal dedicated to the Powyses called la lettre powysienne. We paid tributes to Jacqueline's work on Powys and celebrated her scholarly achievements. Jacqueline's last project was a translation into French of John Cowper's novel Weymouth Sands

Weymouth and Weymouth Sands was also the subject of one of the most interesting lectures at our conference, delivered by Chris Campbell, lecturer in English at Exeter University who discussed the novel and the town, with its stone quarrying background, from a new materialist perspective that gave us all much to think about.

The early history of the Powys Society came under scrutiny again by our Vice-Chairman, David Goodway who presented fuller details of his memory of the origins of the Society 50 years ago when he was present at some of the first meetings. He is, he said, one of the few surviving members from the beginning of the Powys Society.

The annual Llewelyn Powys birthday walk took place on Tuesday 13 August with a small but happy group who met at the Red Lion pub in Winfrith then proceeded to the Sailor's Return in East Chaldon ready to take the walk up to Chydyok farmhouse on Chaldon Down and Llewelyn's monumental stone where flowers were laid. Members listened to readings from Llewelyn's writings as well as readings from the journal of his wife Alyse Gregory. The day concluded with a welcome and refreshing cream tea.

Our last event in 2019 was a discussion of John Cowper's book about Dostoevsky, first published by John Lane in 1947, reprinted by the Village Press in 1974, and led by our Newsletter editor, Kate Kavanagh. The meeting was held at the very appropriately named venue of Pushkin House in central London.

A major project was completed by the Powys Society in 2019 that successfully realized our ambition to ensure the continuing availability of all of John Cowper Powys's major novels.
A Glastonbury Romance, Weymouth Sands, Maiden Castle, Owen Glendower and Porius can now all be acquired as e-books. Early sales figures are very encouraging showing that there is clearly

Members lay flowers at the Powys Memorial on the Birthday Walk world-wide demand by readers for John Cowper's novels.

The Society's Facebook page attracts both members and non-members. All are invited to post new relevant material on our Facebook page. This is the place to go if you wish to exchange views about books by the Powyses with other enthusiasts, join the on-line Powys Reading Group, keep up to date with latest news and Society events or just learn more about the Powyses. The Facebook page helps to supplement our website which includes more details about our publications, associated web-based links and information about how to join the Society. For more information please visit www.powys-society.org , e-mail Hon Secretary at chris.d.thomas@hotmail.co.uk or write to Hon Secretary, Chris Thomas, at 87 Ledbury Road, London W11 2AG.

Our publications programme continues with the production of Newsletters, published three times per year, and an annual scholarly journal all packed with informative details and analysis of the life and works of the Powyses. The Newsletter and Journal are sent free to all members of the Society. Some past Newsletters and the current Newsletter can be downloaded from our website. The annual Powys Journal can also be accessed on-line, in a subscription library, through digital platforms such as ProQuest and JSTOR. A digital version of the Journal can also be read on-line through our web site. Please visit our website for more information. The web site has recently been refreshed and brought up to date by our new web editor, Paul Cheshire, who has done an excellent job to make the site more user friendly, and easier to navigate. It is now possible to search for content. We have also embarked on a project to include more archival material.

We are now planning events in 2020. Details of our meetings and activities will be posted in due course on the Society's website and Facebook page. Our annual conference will take place in Street, near Glastonbury, at the Wessex Hotel, 14-16 August. We are planning lectures on John Cowper Powys and William Blake, on Katie Powys, on Theodore Powys, and on John Cowper Powys's novels A Glastonbury Romance and Rodmoor.

The Powys Society is a recognised charity (801332). The Society was founded in the late 1960s with the aim of promoting public education and recognition of the writings, thought and contribution to the arts of the Powys family, particularly of John Cowper Powys, T.F. Powys and Llewelyn Powys. The Society publishes Newsletters, a Journal as well as books by and about the Powyses, under the imprint The Powys Press, and organises discussion meetings and an annual conference. The Powys Society is international, attracts scholars from around the world, and welcomes anyone interested in learning more about this very talented and unusual family.

Dad's Army in Dorset

By Devina Symes

Some memories of Dorset's Home Guard in WW11 as told to me by my late father, Leslie Burt J.P., and recollection of WW1 which he heard from his grandfather, father, mother and uncles.

In Leslie's words: "The first military memories I have came from my maternal grandfather, Archalaus Whittle, known as Archie, who was born in 1861 at East Knighton, Winfrith. He and his wife, Jane, had ten children and thirty grandchildren.

He told me of his service with the Dorset Volunteers, which he joined at Dorchester Keep in the early 1880s. He recalled that he would go training at a camp near Weymouth, where he was issued with a uniform. On completion of the camp, the uniform had to be handed back, but the men were allowed to keep the hob nailed boots. This, he said, was a God send to him and all the men, and usually lasted until the next camp!
I vividly recall him showing me a tattooed ring on his wedding ring finger – this was for identification purposes should you desert, as some no doubt did – simple but efficient.

My mother, Annie Burt, nee Whittle, who lost her first husband in WW1, told me that she could well remember that while working in service in a house on Weymouth sea front, she was awoken by the sound of bugle calls, summoning the sailors to their ships, and as she looked out of the window could see the whole of the sea front full of sailors running to the harbour side to catch their liberty boat to take them to their ships, which littered the bay.

Three of my mother's brothers were called up in WW1. Having been wounded at the Dardanelles, Uncle Bert was patched up at the Sidney Hall in Weymouth and sent back to the front, but did survive the war.

Uncle Charlie joined the TA before the war and was called up at the outbreak of WW1, where he fought at the Somme, Ypres and Hill 60. He was fortunate to have survived. When coming home on leave from France he told me that he had stopped on top of the hill which overlooked his home at Belhuish, West Lulworth, where, being full of lice, he de-loused himself.

My uncle Sidney Whittle was accidentally drowned in the war, his name is recorded both at West Lulworth War Memorial and in Basra.

In August 1914, mother's other brother, Arthur, who was born in November 1900, was working with his father, Archalaus, (my grandfather) in the valley near Durdle Door; they were preparing latrine's for the troops who were due to camp there on exercise.

On their way to the camp news came through to the troops that War had been declared. Following orders to return to their unit the troops turned round and marched back to Wool station.

A woman verified the facts by telling me how she remembered seeing the soldiers, who were led by a band, marching through the village of Winfrith, and then turning back.

Uncle Arthur was due to be eighteen in November 1918 and he told me how his mother, my grandmother, had received extra cheese rations for him in preparation for his war service. Mercifully, Armistice was called before he could go.

My father, Henry George Burt, known as Jacky, and his three brothers, Thomas, Frederick and James, all farm workers, volunteered to serve their country in WW1. Thankfully they all came home and their names are recorded, along with those killed, on a memorial plaque in St Christopher's church at Winfrith Newburgh, where my father's family can be traced back to the 1500s.

My father, who, like all countrymen, was a very stoic, independent man, said that he served in Greece and France in WW1, and that while in France and desperate for some water he had asked a French woman for some, but was refused.

On returning to the farm the men who had served could often be seen at lunch time scratching bits of pellets from under their skin with their pocket knives, which were very sharp. None ever talked about their ordeal. This stoicism reminds me of the poem, Embarcation, by Thomas Hardy, which he wrote after seeing the Dorset regiment off at Southampton docks in 1899. The lines, 'Non dubious of the cause, non murmering,' sum up the bravery and acceptance of all Dorset soldiers.

In WW2, my father volunteered for the Winfrith Home Guard and was an NCO. He recalled being called out in the middle of the night by the Captain of the Home Guard, the local farmer, who urged him to, take up arms as an invasion was expected. After asking my father if he had a rifle, father replied, "no, only a knobbly stick!" "That'll do, bring it on," said the farmer.

(Who do you think you're kidding Mr Hitler!)
By many blessings the invasion did not happen. Like all people of my father's generation, they lived through ten years of war.

Something else my father told me about the Home Guard was that they would assemble in the village hut (that's what the hall was called in those days) for training and when doing the roll call, after asking the men to remove the cigarettes from behind their ears, the farmer would give out the farm orders for the next day!

Why should England tremble?

DORSET ARCHIVES TRUST

Saving Dorset's Disappearing History

By Sam Johnston and Carola Campbell

Origins and purpose

Dorset Archives Trust (DAT) was founded in 2009. It very much grew out of its predecessor body, the Friends of Dorset's Archives. The latter had been in existence since about 1989 but it was felt that it needed to be refreshed and its aims and objectives reviewed. DAT is a registered charity (number 1000142) with a board of trustees, two patrons and a membership of 150. It supports the work of Dorset History Centre (DHC), the county's archive service based in Dorchester. The latter holds thousands of collections in 43,000 boxes held in climate controlled and protected repositories with records dating from pre-Conquest, Anglo-Saxon charters through to the present day.

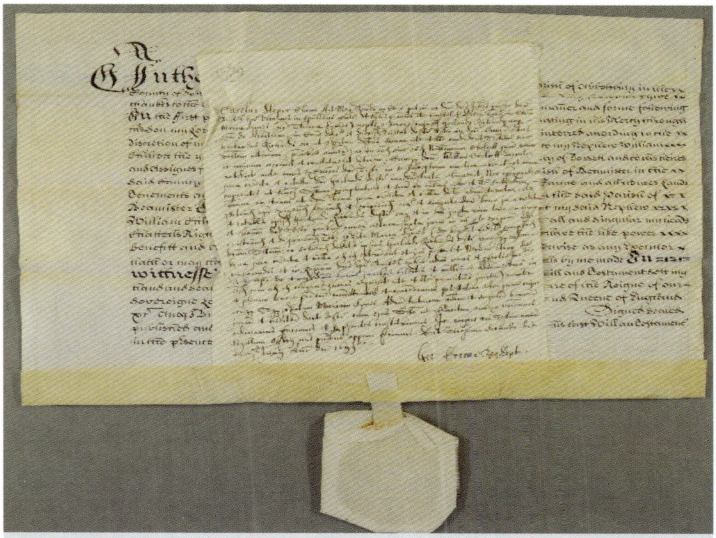

Abbotsbury will, dated 1699, purchased by Dorset Archives Trust, 2018

What are archives?

Archives, at their most basic are social histories: of people's lives, their relationships, health care, social activities; of businesses, their products, employees, finances and taxes; of churches, births, deaths and marriages; of estates, their villages, what they farmed, their household activities – up and downstairs; and so much more. Archives are the records of our past transactions - evidence which can be required for both legal and cultural purposes. Archives are most often found in paper or parchment form but are also photographic material plus film and sound. Increasingly, of course archives can be found in digital form, some have been 'born digitally' and keeping these safe and accessible represents a new major challenge for archive services.

Archive Storage in Dorchester

Most people know archives as they are featured in television documentaries where suitable evidence for a particular action or event is required. Typically, Who Do You Think You Are will use archives to plot an individual's family history e.g. to document their economic fortunes or their health, career or criminal past. Archives also appear in news stories where a new historical perspective has emerged - e.g. when The National Archives declassifies documents each year. Archives remain when living memory starts to fade - seen recently and poignantly in the remembrance of WWI - the images, words and voices of those now deceased who had participated.

Objectives of the Trust

It is true to say that the Trust took several years to really find its feet - to understand how best it could support DHC's work and more generally to promote the recorded heritage of Dorset. Since then, DAT has become a vital part of the way DHC operates and the two organisations are very much aligned in the way they do things with a high degree of mutual interdependency.

DAT's key functions are:

Fundraising - to generate resources to assist with DHC's work and its projects
Advocacy - to promote archives and their value to the wider world

Collections development - to assist in the identification and transfer of relevant archive material

These are closely related and complementary and mean that DAT is able to support the history centre in a wide variety of ways - from encouraging deposits of new records through to submitting applications for grants to a web and social media presence.

Trustees, Patrons and President

Dorset Archives Trust is fortunate to have strong supporters in the Dorset community. The charity's president is Mrs Anthony Pitt-Rivers DL. The board of 11 trustees is chaired by Carola Campbell, wife of Lord Lieutenant Angus Campbell and the charity has two patrons, well-known author and broadcaster Kate Adie and eminent historian Dr Philip Mansel. DAT is a membership organisation and welcomes anyone who supports the preservation of our recorded heritage. Members get priority booking at a reduced rate for events and a free annual event at DHC where they can hear about the year's activities over a glass of wine. More information about the Trust and how to join can be found on its website: www.dorsetarchivestrust.org

DAT trustees meeting HRH Prince of Wales on his visit to DHC in November 2013

Saving Dorset's Disappearing History

DAT has as its strapline 'Saving Dorset's disappearing history'. The latter emerged through a trustee workshop in 2013 where the charity underwent a process of building its core purposes and focusing on outcomes it was seeking to deliver. The strapline very much reflects the vulnerability of archives - items on paper or parchment that can be destroyed by damp, fire, pests or simply thrown away in an effort to create space. One of the key ways in which the Trust helps to save Dorset's History is through its Document Purchase Fund. The Fund exists to allow archives to be purchased at short notice - usually at auction, but sometimes from dealers. The very nature of auctions means that a rapid response is sometimes required. With the Trust's support, DHC has managed to acquire a wide range of archives which would in all probability have been lost to the public collection. These include:

- Archives of the Bond family charting their lives at Tyneham
- Several sets of material relating to Poole Pottery
- WWI Air Raid Precautions archives for Poole
- Archives detailing WW2 bombing raids on Bournemouth
- Archives of Battens, solicitors
- Early Dorset motoring records
- 19th and 20th Dorset-related diaries

The Trust does not have large reserves to draw upon, but when carefully deployed, they can make all the difference between securing archives for public benefit and not.

All the material that has been acquired is available to view at Dorset History Centre. The Trust has also proved critical at helping DHC with its project work. DAT, as a charity is able to access funds from trusts and foundations that are not accessible to a local authority service.

19th century diary - detailing botanical field trips around Dorset - purchased in 2017.

Housing in Boscombe - part of the Cooper- Dean archive at Dorset History Centre.

Bankes Project

The Bankes family of Kingston Lacy and Corfe Castle owned one of the largest estates in Dorset and their incredible archive containing internationally important material was deposited at DHC by the National Trust. The three-year project to catalogue, conserve and promote the archive had strong support from DAT. Over £20,000 was raised by the Trust from external sources. In addition, two fundraising events were held at Kingston Lacy. DAT also played an important role in supporting the project's 60 or so volunteers, hosting annual Christmas lunches to thank them for their important contributions.

Herbert crowdfunding

Another project that DAT supported, and was only possible due to its charitable status was a crowdfunding campaign aimed at raising £8,000 towards completing the job of digitising the photographic archive of Weymouth photographer Graham Herbert. This important archive containing thousands of images charting life in Weymouth and wider Dorset was slowly disappearing due to chemical degradation within the negatives - known as 'vinegar syndrome' due to the pungent smell that is given off. With DAT support and public generosity, the full sum was raised and the archive digitised - so ensuring future access. The Trust was able to benefit from Gift Aid from personal contributions which enhanced the value of the donations.

The Eldridge Pope brewery - from the Graham Herbert photographic archive

Events

The Trust holds a series of events each year - focussed on a speaker, but with tasty food and a glass of wine included in the price of the ticket. Over the years a range of notable speakers have lectured on a wide range of Dorset-related themes - in almost all cases, they are linked to the collections held at DHC. Topics have ranged across railways, the artist Rena Gardiner, Poole Pottery, Dorset landscapes and farming traditions, publishing Dorset-related books to medieval Dorset and the Black Death. The twin purpose of the events is to raise funds for DAT's work on the one hand, and to raise awareness of the collections upon which much of the research in the talks is based. For its summer event, DAT moves around Dorset to various venues having been lucky to host galas at Kingston Lacy, the Hinton St. Mary tithe barn, St. Giles House and most recently, Larmer Tree Gardens.

Guests enjoying a picnic at the DAT summer event at Larmer Tree Gardens

Future plans

Dorset Archives Trust continues to play a vital part in safeguarding and promoting Dorset's heritage. The Trust is involved in several projects which will inform the work of Dorset History Centre over the coming months and years.

Dame Elisabeth Frink

DAT has been gifted the Frink archive - and thereby the records of one of Britain's foremost modern sculptors. This major archive which links DHC to a whole range of UK and foreign museums and galleries hosting Frink's work has led to a project which with the Trust's help has meant that £45,000 has been raised to catalogue, conserve and partially digitise the archive. In addition, DAT will be seeking to raise funds for a museum-grade case in which to exhibit several small Frink pieces which formed part of the bequest. This work will take place in late 2019.

Dame Elisabeth Frink in her studio at Woolland (from the Frink archive at Dorset History Centre)

Capital project

DAT has long supported DHC's key challenge - the decreasing amount of space that it has in which to house new archival deposits. The History Centre, erected in 1991 had an anticipated accrual space of 25 years which it has now well exceeded. The service has been working for some years to secure funding to allow new strong rooms to be added to the existing building. DAT's role is crucial in helping to fundraise for this major project - both from trusts and foundations, but from private philanthropy. We are hopeful that the project will move forward in the near future and it remains the service's key priority.

Student travel fund

On a much more modest, but nevertheless very useful level, DAT has allocated a small fund which will allow students to claim travel expenses to enable them to come to DHC to access and research Dorset's archives. The Trust is keen to encourage young people's interest in history and this has been identified as a real need as hard-pressed students often do not have the funds to undertake even modest journeys.

In conclusion

As can be seen, Dorset Archives Trust plays a crucial role in helping to preserve and promote Dorset's recorded heritage - the sometimes lesser-known heritage without which we would not be able to interrogate and understand the past. Like all charities, it depends on a core of dedicated trustees and a loyal membership to deliver its priorities and maintain momentum.

If you are interested in history or just want to know more, the Trust welcomes new members and it encourages all interested parties to consider how they can play their part in saving Dorset's disappearing history.

To learn more, join or donate, please see: www.dorsetarchivestrust.org

Sam Johnston, Secretary, Dorset Archives Trust
Carola Campbell, Chairman, Dorset Archives Trust

Sea Blues (Old and New)

Judi Moore

I was an exile from the sea for many years
somewhere where no sea breezes could blow,
no salt rime fog glass, no sand invade
sandals and sandwiches. On this island Britain
you cannot get further from the sea
whichever way you travel than where
my life beached. My soul shrivelled.

I took each opportunity I could to return
to the sea's salt lick, so its lithe power
could rehydrate tissues desiccated from the lack of it.
I spent my holidays on Grecian islands
surrounded by the sea, where the light is
pure and clear and clean. Where I could
suck up the colours of the Aegean, reciting
them in my head (and now here): turquoise, azure,
Prussian, cobalt, sapphire, bottle green,
aquamarine, jade and eau de nil ;
writhing sea mists there are baby blue
so pale they're almost white; sometimes a pinkness
marks the edges between land and sea,
pale as Aphrodite's veil of thinnest stuff.

Now the sea is just a few steps from
my English seaside home. It lubricates my life.
It breathes in and out like I do, with every wave and tide.
I see it every day. Each morning. Every night.
I greet it like the old friend that it is.

For here are the blues I missed so much,
not quite as dazzling in our northern light.
These are more metallic hues
than I have loved in waters further south.
Here is the hammered pewter sea which lies
under a dull, still day. Storms whip up breakers
the colour of an iron bar, tipped with lace.
On nights when the moon is full there is a liquid path
of mercury which leads, like a siren song, to the horizon.
And sometimes – magical enough to make me
hold my breath – there is a Lalique-lilac sea at dawn, or twilight,
its tiny ripples motionless as glass.

My exile now has ended: I am home.

Stalbridge For Sale

By Hilary Townsend

In 2018 the United Kingdom marked the end of the Great War and the Armistice in 1918. This was done very thoroughly in Stalbridge but we also had another great centenary to mark. It was 100 years since the sale of the Stalbridge Estate. Early in1918 the owner, Lord Stalbridge, had decided to sell his huge estate. This meant some 200 houses, shops, farms, allotments and fields in Stalbridge were put up for auction that September. Lord Stalbridge was in the army at the time and still on active service in France, so he was obliged to sell the estate in this way.

A member of the Committee volunteered to lead the project and for nearly two years the Stalbridge History Society researched the Sale. The research also aimed to provide a snapshot of daily life in the village at that time - life in the church, the school, pubs, businesses and in the streets. The 1911 census was used and the 1920 electoral roll and a few copies of the original sale catalogue still survived. My father had attended the sale, carefully marking up on his copy the names of the buyers and the money they paid for their properties. At the same time, the catalogue listed who the original owners were. In this way we acquired a great deal of information about the properties, the tenants and what Stalbridge was like at the time; and a local genealogist transcribed and printed copies of the sale catalogue for us.

This exhibition was the most expensive thing The History Society had ever attempted. Stalbridge Hall was booked but we had to raise the hire charges, liability insurance premium and many other costs. Our Heritage Lottery Fund application was unsuccessful but in every other way we were incredibly lucky. We raised some money by crowdfunding, then, as the project became known, we gained tremendous financial support from businesses, local residents and Stalbridge Town Council.

Exhibition Flyer

Support from the Society's members poured in, with offers of research, writing, storing display boards we had been given, planning, stewarding and refreshments. We received valuable help from the Dorset Heritage Centre and the local museums adviser about how to set up such an exhibition. We were also exceptionally fortunate to enlist the services of a graphic design and print expert who lived locally. He was absolutely dedicated and his enthusiasm and hard work were invaluable to the Exhibition.

Finally, the Exhibition's opening times were fixed from Saturday, 1st September to Tuesday, 4th September 2018, including the actual Centenary. Planning to open the Exhibition over the weekend greatly increased attendance. Flyers were printed for Stalbridge for Sale and widely distributed. Members were asked to help with stewarding, printing out bits of sale catalogue on request, looking up names on online genealogical sites, welcoming people, encouraging donations and baking lots of cakes to offer visitors. In addition, a local biscuit factory offered us a very generous selection of their goods.

The press coverage of the event was amazing. Our local Blackmore Vale Magazine, based in Stalbridge High Street then, gave us excellent coverage. We had researched its own property, at the time of the sale occupied by a family of tailors and included in the sale, which the BVM was delighted to print. The story was picked up by the magazine of the popular Who Do You Think You Are? BBC programme. This was an excellent piece of luck, giving the Exhibition very wide coverage. Our graphic designer had created a series of large posters using the information we had gathered and these posters were impressive. In addition, we created a series of A4 sheets for each of the over 200 properties, and Stalbridge Archive Society provided us with invaluable original documents and maps.

Exhibition Stands

The sheer hard work and planning by everyone connected with the Exhibition resulted in the utter professionalism of the final event. It was clear, well organised and with a route to direct viewers through it. The response was overwhelming. So many local families had been affected by the Sale in 1918. The excellent publicity made it well known and over 1,000 people visited, sometimes from very far away. We were particularly touched by the sheer good humour of everyone involved. The co-operation and enthusiasm were unfailing and there was a real sense of community. People came together in a common cause. They met old friends, in some cases relations they didn't know existed, and were delighted to find so much information about Stalbridge a hundred years ago.

The Society had agonised about the cost of this expensive undertaking but it was soon clear that the generous response meant all our costs would be safely covered. There have been many enquiries since about people and properties and from another History Society asking for our advice. All the photographs and information have been carefully filed and it is hoped eventually to bring out a book on the subject. Stalbridge History Society is delighted to find that its hard work and dedication have produced such a response to this auction of the sale of Stalbridge 100 years ago –Our Sale of the Century.

Home Thoughts from Abroad

David Kirkpatrick

'Wear the Absence' - these words were mentioned in a sermon at our church in Charlotte, NC in America. On All Saints Day, we honour the memory of all members who have passed during the year. It is a moment of feeling great loss and sadness but also of remembrance.

When we wear the absence, it is our attempt to think and feel a connection to those who have passed on. We celebrate what we have experienced and continue to experience from our memory of them. We wear our thoughts and feelings every day to cherish the importance of that person in our lives.

In 1904, our founder William Watkins was wearing the absence for Dorset as he gathered like- minded men to his office. The society was their attempt to continue feeling connected to the county they loved. Having this supportive society must have been a great comfort to the members to share their experiences of Dorset while they pursued their work in London.

For 19 years, my wife and I have had the pleasure to own Old Gaol Cottage in Cerne Abbas. Though we are in residence only part of the year, it is our Dorset home. Many friends ask me how often we are in our village. My response is every day. Dorset is not just a place to visit. It is an important part of defining who we are.

So, the Society continues to play an important role today as it did in 1904. Regardless of where our lives take us, it is a way to feel connected to the most beautiful part of the county. That is why my membership in the Society of Dorset Men means so much to me. It helps me wear the absence for Dorset.

(Editor's Note - David and his wife Jan always try to be with us for our County Dinner each year but as we go to press David has emailed to say that sadly they have other commitments this year. However, he has also sent this splendid photo of his Mini-Cooper with its North Carolina number plate proudly advertising our county and sporting our badge in its rear window. "Home thoughts from abroad" with a vengeance!)

Keep Remembering

Christopher Jary

Having spent the five years 2014-2018 remembering the First World War, this year at the Keep Military Museum we turned our attention to several important 75th anniversaries from the Second. With these in mind – and with some welcome financial support from our Regiments and the Cooper-Dean Foundation – we closed from Christmas 2018 until mid-February 2019 to instal our new Second World War Gallery. Our aim was to tell some of our Regiments' stories more vividly through the stories of individual soldiers.

The new Gallery starts with a timeline, showing the major events and the Regiments' campaigns from 1939-45. Beside it is a world map displaying the campaign stars and medals and showing where they were earned. Opposite is the first display case, describing how the 2nd Dorsets – the first to go to war in September 1939 – fought a heroic rearguard action on the La Bassée Canal to allow the rest of their Division to escape. The Dorsets were expected to be killed or captured but their Commanding Officer, Colonel Steve, planned otherwise. Compass in hand and with his Second in Command, Tom Molloy, beside him with a map, he personally led his 245 survivors back – across the line of the German advance behind them, and across canals, rivers, fences – until they caught up with the British retreat. It is an inspiring story from the dark days of defeat and it set a high standard of leadership, determination and courage for the Dorsets to follow throughout the war.

Beside it stands a case remembering the 1st Dorsets' and 2nd Devons' war in the Mediterranean: first their years on starved, bombed, beleaguered Malta throughout their bitter siege 1940-43, then in six weeks of vicious battles under a blazing summer sun on Sicily and finally landing on the toe of Italy to speed Monty's advance to Salerno. This case tells the story of our Regiments' part in the turning point of the war, when the Allies turned to the offensive and the liberation of Continental Europe began.

A large case remembers the same Battalions leading the D-Day landings at 0730 on 6th June 1944. The 1st Dorsets and 1st Hampshires, side by side, were the first British infantry ashore that day. This was the beginning of the end for Hitler's Germany and this case shows how our Malta Brigade (Devons, Dorsets and Hampshires), wearing their scarlet and white Maltese Cross, led the invasion. The story is personalised by a film based on the illicit diary of Private Terry Parker of 18 Platoon of the 1st Dorsets. The case also remembers the battle of attrition that was the three-month Normandy Campaign and the gallant, sacrificial part played in it by 43rd Wessex Division, which included the 4th and 5th Dorsets and the Dorset Yeomen of the 94th Field Regiment, Royal Artillery. No Division ever fought harder than the 43rd in a campaign whose casualties rivalled those on the Somme. Another film remembers their horrific losses on Hill 112 and includes a recent interview with 98-year-old Ron Beale of the 4th Dorsets while a board tells the story of Captain Denis Clark MC of the 94th Field Regiment at Mont Pincon.

Round the corner, our largest case tells the story of the Forgotten Army, who fought a savage, relentless enemy in the jungles of Assam and Burma. These are the men – the 1st Devons and 2nd Dorsets – who turned defeat into victory at Imphal and Kohima and then chased a defeated Japanese army south towards Rangoon. Here their proud story is remembered and vividly described with the help of a contemporary film made during the Dorsets' bloody battle around the tennis court at Kohima. The Dorsets' remarkable, fearless Padre, Gus Claxton MC, is remembered with pride and affection.

A new case tells the proud story of the contribution made to victory by the women of Dorset while a second provides an atmospheric display depicting wartime life here in blitzed Britain. Both are the work of our new Curator, Laura Gardner, who has led the Museum since May 2019. They add an important new dimension to our story.

Our last case describes the rest of the campaign in North West Europe: the ill-fated operation that failed to hold Arnhem bridge, the crossing of the Rhine and the final surrender of Nazi Germany in May 1945. Beside it, appropriately, stands Hitler's desk, brought back from Occupied Berlin by a Dorset general who acquired it from a Russian counterpart.

During the year we have so far used our new Gallery to mark two anniversaries. On 13th May we remembered the victory at Kohima with a tea party for the families of veterans. On 8th June we played a major part in Dorchester's commemoration of the 75th anniversary and launched our new book, "D-Day Spearhead Brigade", which tells the story of the Hampshires, Dorsets and Devons on D-Day. Made by Claire Vera, our three new short films (of Kohima, D-Day and Hill 112) are constantly showing in our Gallery and (as I write this) we are making a fourth telling the story of our Regiments' part at Arnhem. There will be more films to come – on a range of subjects.

WW2 Gallery
Copyright: Keep Military Museum

Next year the anniversaries will continue. March will mark the Crossing of the Rhine, when the 2nd Devons, 4th and 5th Dorsets and 94th Field Regiment crossed by boat and the 12th Devons arrived by glider. VE-Day and VJ-Day will follow. These victories, which preserved the liberties we enjoy today, are the cornerstones of modern history. They were bought with the blood of our parents and grandparents and our job is to ensure their courage and sacrifice are remembered.

But the Keep is not just about the two world wars. May 2020 will also see the 25th anniversary of the deployment of the 1st Devonshire and Dorsets to peace-keeping duties in Bosnia. We are therefore planning some events and a small exhibition to mark this more recent anniversary and to record and preserve the memories of our soldiers who served there. From 1700 to 2007 we have plenty to remember and a wealth of good stories to tell. Do come and see us.

CRIES FOR DORCHESTER

Alistair Chisholm

Many readers will be aware of the proposal to develop a large area of downland immediately to the north of Dorchester. Included within the site are the Blue Bridge and quite a length of the Frome Valley, The Dorset County Showground and extensive downland up to Waterston Ridge. The plan is for 3500 houses to be built.

There is a lot of concern within the town and local people have formed a group called STAND – Save The Area North of Dorchester – to counter the proposal. STAND is supported by CPRE.

This is a current local issue and as Town Crier I deliver cries on a wide range of subjects of topical interest.

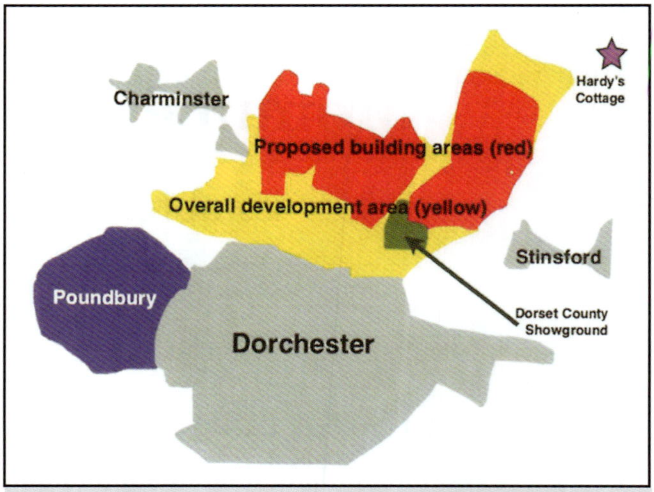

Outline Map of the Plan

In his novel The Mayor of Casterbridge Hardy described Dorchester as being "like a chessboard on a green table-cloth" and these words remain very apt today:

A Cry for STAND *(These words of Hardy still apply):*

For to the north lie fields and sky.
Town and down both meet right here,
A Roman edge that's still most dear.......

The countryside from the pump you see,
So close, so green, what a USP!
Paths and bridleways criss-cross this land,
An area so special we MUST make a STAND.

For should it be lost, 'twill change Dorch. For ever,
Come, let's STAND together and cry loudly, "NEVER!"
GOD SAVE THE QUEEN

AND ANOTHER:

OYEZ! OYEZ! OYEZ!
'Twill be sad enough to lose the view,
The loss of farmland we shall rue.
They'll not be building homes we need,
For their concern is to feed their greed.
We've saved this town in times long passed,
Let's do it again and ensure it lasts.
GOD SAVE THE QUEEN

AND A THIRD:

OYEZ! OYEZ! OYEZ.
We are facing our finale, if we lose our northern edge,
If we lose this open country with each tree and ancient hedge.
We are the only Roman town with an edge that's stayed the same;
Should we despoil two thousand years? Do you believe we'll gain?
A few will make a fortune, but what's in it for us?
Promises are plentiful, but often turn to dust.
Must we accept what we are told? Do our views matter not?
Tell Dorset Council what you think – this development's a blot.
Our story and our setting are singularly fine,
Against this desecration gird up your loins and sign.
GOD SAVE THE QUEEN

AND LASTLY:

OYEZ! OYEZ! OYEZ!
People of Dorchester heed my words,
For we could lose our wildlife and birds.
What's in it for us if they build to the north?
More traffic, more pressure, what good will come forth?
Are we to pay the ultimate price
For profit, for gain, for greed that's a vice?
Landowners and developers promise the world,
But their profit comes first, good intentions oft hurled.
The setting of our town is a truly unique feature
We must fight for every field, every hedge and every creature.
For once it's gone it's gone for good and never will return
Should this happen on our watch? When will we ever learn?
GOD SAVE THE QUEEN

STAND's website is www.stand-dorchester.net

(Editor's Note: Alistair has been Dorchester's famous Town Crier for some twenty years and has won many town crying competitions. He is also an accomplished local historian and has a most detailed knowledge of the history of Dorchester. Any views or opinions contained within the above article are not those of The Society of Dorset Men. As a society we do not hold or express views or opinions on this or other issues.)

COUNTY DINNER 2019

Our County Dinner was once again held at the George Albert Hotel, Evershot on Saturday 26th October, attended by a rather disappointing number of members, together with wives and partners. This traditional event, known as the "Annual Veast" has been a feature of the Society calendar for 115 years. Our President, Lord Fellowes of West Stafford and his wife Lady Emma Fellowes presided and warmly welcomed everyone as they arrived. Our principal guests this year were Mr James Gibson Fleming, the Deputy Lord Lieutenant. Mr Philip Warr, The High Sheriff and His Honour Judge Mark Lucraft QC. the Chief Coroner for England and Wales. During the dinner the usual toasts were proposed amongst which was one for those who served our Country and one to our ladies. Everyone enjoyed an excellent dinner served by the waiting staff with speed and precision! Mr Alistair Chisholm, the Town Crier of Dorchester, acted as Master of Ceremonies with humour and aplomb; his powerful voice meant that he did not require the use of a microphone!

Before the cheese course was served, the traditional ceremony which includes the Blue Vinny cheese being paraded to the tune "Maid of Glenconell", the regimental march of the old Dorset Regiment, then tasted by the President, was performed.

Another of our traditions over the years has been to send a dialect message of loyal greetings to HM The Queen and this year it was as follows:-
"Yer Majesty - We members o' the Zociety o' Darzet Men voregathered ver our yerly veast at the Jarge Albert'otel down yer in Darzet d'zend yer Majesty our artvelt greetins an' expression o' loyal zupport. We'd pray that midst th' unzettlements that bezet us yer majesty will be vouchsafed the vullest measure o' 'ealth 'an 'appiness. I d' bide yer Majesty's vaithvul zarvent Julian Vellowes, The Lard Vellowes o' West Stafford Prezident o' the Zociety o' Darzet Men"

The following reply was received from the Private Secretary to HM The Queen, "The Queen was pleased to receive your thoughtful message of loyalty on behalf of the Society of Dorset Men sent on the occasion of your Yearly Feast which is being held at the George Albert Hotel. Her Majesty much appreciates your kind words and, in return, asked me to send her warm good wishes to all concerned for a most enjoyable evening".

The Hambro Cup was then presented by the President to Neil Gatehouse for winning the golf tournament recently held at Came Down Golf Club, Dorchester.

Our guest speaker, His Honour Judge Mark Lucraft QC then addressed the gathering. He gave a most interesting talk concerning his family connections with the County and enjoyable holidays spent when visiting as a small boy. He then gave an account of his career and his eventual appointment as a High Court Judge. As Coroner he has been involved in some of the high-profile inquests in London concerning terrorist incidents, highlighting two incidents of bravery resulting in the award of the George Cross. He concluded his talk by proposing the toast "Dorset our County".

The President responded and made mention of the fact that we should not forget during our present troubled times, how fortunate we are to live in the beautiful County of Dorset.

Our President and Lady Fellowes with our Guests

Photo by Trevor Matthews

BOOK REVIEWS

SAS Italian Job

The Secret Mission to Storm a Forbidden Nazi Fortress

Damien Lewis

Published by Quercus - £20.00

Michael Lees was a true son of Dorset, the grandson of Sir Elliot Lees, 1st Baronet, of South Lytchett Manor. From school he followed his father into the Dorset Yeomanry and the outbreak of war found him drafted to India where he wangled his way into the Parachute Brigade. Later, in Cairo and desperate for action, he talked his way into the Yugoslav section of SOE and was dropped into that country where he carried out acts of sabotage and found himself on the wrong side of British Government policy by championing Mihailovic's Cetniks against their sworn enemies, the partisans who fought with Tito. The story of this period is told in Michael's own book 'Special Operations Executed' published in 1986.

After leaving Yugoslavia, Michael was inserted into Italy where he was British Liaison Officer in the Reggia region, and when, in late 1944, a proposal was made to drop in a force of 50 SAS men he was the only one to make a positive response. The result was an audacious attack on the Headquarters of the German LI Gebergs (Mountain) Corps at

Villa Rossi, a key component of the Gothic Line which would have to be crossed the give the Allies victory in Italy.

Now a new book by that foremost of recorders of military history, Damien Lewis, has set out the story of that raid. Damien writes in clear prose and at a rollicking pace which places the reader at the heart of the action and feeling almost part of it. Using files which have been declassified for the purpose of writing his book, he also calls on authentic eyewitness testimony and the recollections of family members to reveal 'an untold epic of daring, ruthless rule breaking and shocking betrayal'.

The betrayal referred to is the extraordinary decision not to award Lees a DSO or even an MC. Neither was he promoted to major, even though the attack he originated must rate as one of the most ambitious and daring operations carried out by resistance forces. A petition to right this wrong exists and can be accessed by visiting: - https://www.change.org/p/parliament-to-debate-reinstating-mc-award-military-cross-to-captain-michael-lees-that-was-wrongly-denied-in-wwii

This is a book that is difficult to put down and I recommend it to all who like military history. Damien Lewis is to be congratulated on documenting in such fine style an action which, if written as a work of fiction, would be impossible to believe. That the central character is Michael 'Wild Man' Lees, who as a son of Dorset, is 'one of us' gives an added incentive to devour it.

Reviewed by Peter Lush

Wimborne Minster - Portrait of a Town by Alan Bennett

Review by Hayne Russell

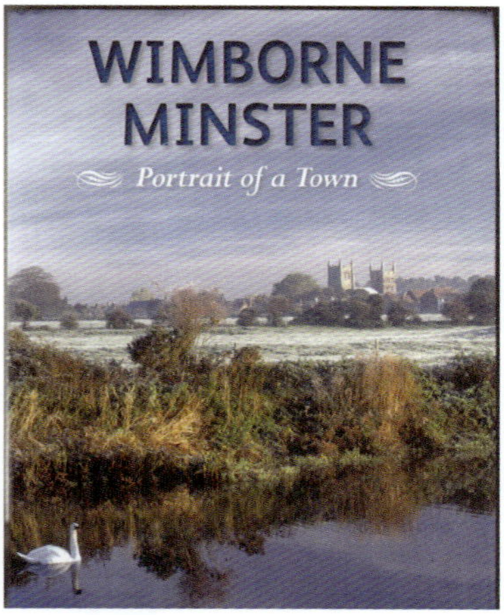

Although this is a book which will appeal mainly to those connected with, or living in, Wimborne it will also be of interest to those who appreciate a book full of fascinating facts about people and places, and the history and events associated with a small Dorset town. The author Alan Bennett is a member of our Society, and he's spent three years painstakingly researching the content of his book. This is reflected in the wealth of information and wonderful photographs within its covers. It spans not quite two years in the life of the town, touches on many aspects and both entertains and informs the reader. This is a book to pick up and put down but each time you'll find something new and interesting.

The cover price is £20 and the book is available from Gulliver's of Wimborne, Wimborne Tourist Information Centre, The Minster Bookshop and Pamphill Dairy Farm Shop. The author is donating £2 from every copy sold to be divided between The Friends of Victoria Hospital Wimborne and The Wimborne Dementia Friendly Community.

BOOK REVIEW

D-Day Spearhead Brigade: The Hampshires, Dorsets and Devons on 6th June 1944

By Christopher Jary

Christopher Jary, that indefatigable chronicler of the actions of the county regiment, has done it again. 'D-Day Spearhead Brigade' is a sequel to 'Yells, Bells & Smells' which recounted the story of the experience of the Hampshires, Dorsets and Devons during the Siege of Malta, and Christopher has reassembled his team of aides and researchers – Nick Speakman, James Porter, Andrew Edwards and Laurence Thornton-Grimes – to produce a minute by minute account of the three Battalions on D-day when they seized and secured a bridgehead above Bayeux.

Divided into chapters each covering a few hours of the day's action, the book is based on the testimony of eighty-three survivors and an immediacy is given to the narrative by the simple device of seamlessly stitching their memories into Christopher's own text. The effect is to place the reader at the heart of the action and for those of us who have visited the scene and know the terrain (and I am sure there are many) you can almost smell the cordite. By the same token we find the names of the officers and men becoming so familiar that they appear, if not yet as friends, at least as acquaintances.

The term 'Spearhead Brigade' was hard earned and was a compliment accorded by Montgomery himself who, having visited them in Malta and been impressed with their state of readiness, chose them for the invasion of Sicily and then the toe of Italy. He again insisted that the Brigade should spearhead the Normandy landings. Compliment it may have been, but fraught with danger for the recipients. They were not to let him down.

Christopher Jary's style and command of the English language shines throughout this book so that, although it is heavy on detail, it is light on presentation making it an easy read and difficult to put down as the action proceeds at pace from one scene of combat to another. There is a wealth of easy-to-read maps and diagrams and the sacrifice and bravery of that single day is rounded off with a chapter on the 'unfinished business' of D+1 – D+4 and put into context with a Postscript of 'What lay ahead: D+4 to VE-Day and beyond.' Also included are many Appendices listing Orders of Battle, Rolls of Honour and Gallantry Awards.

D-Day was a triumph that has since shaped all our lives and whilst this book is a must-read for all lovers of Dorset that rejoice in the achievements of the county regiment, it should be read by a much wider audience who owe, in no small part, their present freedom to a day that turned the course of the Second World War.

Reviewed by Peter Lush

D-Day Spearhead Brigade is available from Waterstones or other bookshops for £22 and from the Keep for £18 (£21 with postage within the UK).

A Note from the Editor

This is my first year as editor of The Year Book and I feel proud and privileged to have been appointed. I'm still relatively "new" to Dorset, having moved here from East Anglia in 2003, and I'm actually a native of Colchester – that's as a person rather than an oyster! I hope that one day I'll become accepted at least as a "Dorset local" but I'm still not sure about how long this might take.

Even so, my connection with Dorset goes back to 1966 when I proposed marriage to a young lass from Yorkshire when we found ourselves lost in the County whilst driving back to Surrey from a stay in Devon. To commemorate this event we spent our subsequent honeymoon in Lyme Regis! Over later years we consolidated our familiarity with Dorset through frequent visits to close friends and family in Gillingham, Bridport and Bournemouth, and to holidays in Purbeck, and so, over quite a while, I've got to know the County rather well. Also, as our Society's constitution says, membership is open to those who have connection by birth, descent, marriage or property, so I reckon I'm well qualified!

It's a delight to be your editor and I'm most grateful to all the authors and others who have contributed loads of most interesting articles, poems, pieces and pictures of such quality that I really haven't had to edit very much at all. Thank you to all stalwart regular contributors and to quite a few newcomers, some of whom protested that "they couldn't write" until I showed them how to hold and manipulate a Biro pen! Again, thank you all and thank you especially to Chris Smith of Print Team, who has been absolutely indispensable in giving his total co-operation and lending his unparalleled professional expertise to the design and layout of our book.

I ask all contributors, members and other readers to please keep sending in your articles, poems, pieces and pictures so that our Year Book might continue into 2021 and for many years to come.

Thank you everyone.

Nicholas Wright

IN MEMORIAM

The President and Members mourn the loss of the following worthy fellow Dorsets and tender sincere sympathy to their relatives:

JAMES RUTTER (Shaftesbury)	Member	Dec 2017
SIDNEY HANNAM (Spetisbury)	Vice President	1/11/18
JOHN HEATHER (Portland) (Society Web Master)	Hon Life Member	21/11/18
DAVID GRAHAM (Weymouth)	Vice President	1/4/18
PETER STORRS (Weymouth)	Member	6/5/18
DAVID HODDER (Dorchester)	Member	18/12/18
LEONARD CHICK MBE (Poole)	Life Member	16/1/19
M R STILL (Dorchester)	Member	4/2/19
ANTHONY YEATMAN JP DL (Corfe Mullen)	Life Member	18/2/19
BRIAN ELTON (Dorchester)	Member	28/2/19
ANTHONY ROWE (Wimborne)	Life Member	28/9/18
DR G W TAPPER (Shaftesbury)	Member	14/3/19
M JEFFREY (Shaftesbury)	Member	15/3/19
R D KNIGHT (Poole)	Member	1/10/18
J G M LAMB (Pimperne)	Member	10/1/19
M J RANGER (Swanage)	Member	26/3/19
RAYMOND STONE (Portland) (Committee Member 1982-2011)	Vice President	6/4/19
JOHN HAMBLIN (Wimborne)	Member	12/4/19
A F H LANE (Melcombe Bingham)	Member	26/1/19
G M J NORTHOVER (Corfe Castle) Life Member		2/7/19
LESLIE KEATS (Parkstone)	Member	10/5/19
MICHAEL GWINN (Dorset)	Life Member	30/4/19
DAVID JONES (Winterborne Zelston)	Member	1/5/19
ROBIN HUSSEY (Gillingham)	Member	20/9/19
GORDON NEALE (Gillingham)	Member	20/9/19
RALPH JERRAM (Gillingham)	Member	20/9/19
GEOFFREY COFFIN (Bailie Gate) (Secretary, Purbeck Branch for many years)	Member	24/9/19
RAYMOND SMITH MBE (Branksome)	Member	21/9/19

"WHO'S A-FEAR'D?"

'A Silver Tower Dorset Red Banner Bears'

RULES OF THE SOCIETY

(Incorporating the alterations passed at the Special General Meeting of the Society held on 28th April 2019)

NAME

1. The name of the Society shall be **"THE SOCIETY OF DORSET MEN"**

OBJECTS

2 The objects of the Society shall be: To make and renew personal friendships and associations, to promote good fellowship among Dorset men wherever they may reside, to foster love of County and pride in its history and traditions and to assist by every means in its power, natives of Dorset who may stand in need of the influence and help of the Society.

MEMBERSHIP

3 The Society shall consist of a President, Deputy Presidents, Honorary Life Members, Life Members and Members.

QUALIFICATIONS

4 Any person connected with the County of Dorset by birth, descent marriage, property or past or present residence in the County shall be eligible to be elected to the membership.

MODE OF ELECTION AND TERMINATION OF MEMBERSHIP

5 (i) The names of all candidates for election shall be submitted to the Committee, who shall have full power to deal with the same.

(ii) The Committee shall have the power to remove from the list, the name of any Member whose subscription is in arrears for two years.

(iii) The Committee may also at any time in their discretion terminate the membership of any person without furnishing reasons for their action, in which event a pro rata proportion of the subscription will be returned.

SUBSCRIPTIONS

6 The Subscriptions to the Society shall be:

(a) Life Member - one payment £200.00

(b) Members per annum (payable 1st October) £15.00

The subscriptions will apply whether the member is residing in the U.K. or Overseas.

OFFICERS

7 (i) The Officers of the Society shall be:

Chairman, Deputy Chairman, Honorary Secretary. Honorary Membership Secretary, Honorary Treasurer, Honorary Year Book Editor, Honorary Newsletter Editor and they together with the President and Deputy Presidents, if desired, shall be elected at the Annual General Meeting each year.

(ii) The committee shall have the power to fill any vacancy arising during the year.

COMMITTEE

8 (i) The Society shall be governed by a Committee not exceeding fifteen in number, to be elected from the Members at the Annual General Meeting. In addition, the Officers of the Society shall be

ex-officio Members of the Committee. Seven shall form a quorum.

(ii) The Committee may delegate any of their powers to a Sub-committee.

(iii) The Committee shall retire annually, but shall be eligible for re-election.

(iv) Not less than twelve days before the Annual General Meeting the Honorary Secretary shall send to every Member a notice of the Meeting. The Notice shall also intimate to the Members that any two Members may nominate one or more Members for election as Officer or to the Committee, and that such nomination must be sent to the Honorary Secretary not less than four days before the Meeting.

MEETINGS

9 (i) The Annual General Meeting will be held on a date to be decided by the Committee.

(ii) The Committee may at any time convene a Special General Meeting and shall do so within six weeks of the Honorary Secretary receiving a written requisition signed by twenty Members. This should state the subject or subjects to be discussed and the resolution. Notice of the date and place of all Special Meetings shall be sent by the Honorary Secretary to each Member twelve clear days prior to the date fixed and shall state the object or purpose for which such a Meeting is convened.

BOOKS AND RECORDS TO BE KEPT

10 Proper Books of Accounts showing all income and expenditure shall be kept by the Honorary Treasurer, and the Honorary Secretary shall record and keep Minutes of all Meetings of the Committee. The Membership Secretary shall record and maintain a list of Members under the provisions of the General Data Protection Regulations.

EXAMINATION OF ACCOUNTS

11 At each Annual General Meeting two Examiners shall be elected to examine the Accounts of the Society for presentation to the Members at the next Annual General Meeting.

ALTERATION OF RULES

12 These Rules may be amended, altered or varied by a majority of two thirds of the Members voting at the Annual General Meeting or at a Special General Meeting.

COMMITTEE CHAIRMAN

STUART ADAM
Court Barton, West Bagber, Taunton. TA4 3EQ. Tel. (01823) 432076
Email: stu.adam@outlook.com

DEPUTY COMMITTEE CHAIRMAN

ANDREW PROWSE
Links View, 62 Field Barn Drive, Weymouth, DT4 0EE.
Tel. (01305)779988
Email: Andrew.prowse@tiscali.co.uk

MEMBERS OF COMMITTEE:

DOUGLAS BEAZER, TOM CRABBE, SHAUN CREGAN,
ANDREW HUTCHINGS, JOHN ROUSELL, SAM WOODCOCK

OFFICERS:

Hon. Secretary: Hayne Russell
34 Brunel Drive, Preston, Weymouth DT3 6NX
Tel: (01305) 833700
Email: hrussell@gotadsl.co.uk

Hon. Assistant and Membership Secretary: Peter Lush
25 Maumbury Square, Dorchester, DT1 1TY
Tel: (01305) 260039
Email: membership@societyofdorsetmen.co.uk

Hon. Treasurer: Ian Morton
1 Wainwright Close, Preston, Weymouth, DT3 6NS
Tel: (01305) 832722
Email: ianvalmorton@fsmail.net

Hon. Editor "The Dorset Year Book": Nicholas Wright
39 Cross Road, Weymouth, DT4 9QX
Tel: (01305) 459268
Email: wright1941@btinternet.com

Hon. Newsletter Editor: John Neimer
Rowan House, 26 Corfe Road, Stoborough, BH20 5AB
Tel: (01929) 552622
Email: john@jandpneimer.plus.com

Society Archivist and Historian: Rev. Dr. John Travell
44 Cornwall Road, Dorchester, DT1 1RY
Tel: (01305) 264681
Email: johntravell@outlook.com